Six Myths We Live By

6 Myths We Live By

And How to Overcome Them

Karuna Cayton

Wisdom Publications
132 Perry Street
New York, NY 10014 USA
wisdom.org

Library of Congress Cataloging-in-Publication Data is available.
LCCN 2025013273

ISBN 978-1-61429-876-2 ebook ISBN 978-1-61429-884-7

29 28 27 26 25
5 4 3 2 1

Author photo by Capucine T. Dekyong. Cover design by Marc Whitaker.
Interior design by Tony Lulek.

Printed on acid-free paper that meets the guidelines for permanence and durability of the Production Guidelines for Book Longevity of the Council on Library Resources.

Printed in the United States of America.

Please visit fscus.org.

Contents

Introduction

After the Buddha gained enlightenment under the Bodhi Tree, he didn't teach for seven weeks. He didn't even speak. He thought, "I can't communicate this. Others won't get it." His fellow ascetics kept requesting that he teach, and when he finally did, the first thing he taught was the four noble truths, beginning with the first truth: life is suffering.

From our modern perspective it might seem odd to start there. What a bummer! Life is suffering? Why didn't he start with the truth of nirvana, the liberation from all suffering, something more uplifting? That's how we would do it in our culture: Make a promise to consumers, a carrot on the end of the stick to lead them through a necessary set of actions so they can arrive at a place of greater understanding. The Buddha, on the other hand, started with the truth of suffering because things, frankly, are not that good. If you don't have an appreciation for our human condition—whether you call it suffering, incompleteness, or discontent—you won't make the real effort that is required for true peacefulness. True peacefulness is often referred to as "nirvana" or "enlightenment." This is called "true" because it never ends or is uprooted by the many emotional and mental disorders that typically run our life. When we say we're at peace, it is not really "true peace," because before too long it will wane and be replaced by some sort of unstable attitude or mindset.

The Buddha's teachings have been at home in Asian societies for over two millennia, and have only begun to be introduced into Western cultures earnestly over the past several decades. With respect to the presentation of Buddhist thought in the modern world, a lot of it is what I might call "watered-down milk." When I was living in Nepal, if we couldn't get our milk directly from a farmer, we would buy it in the marketplace. The big challenge there was getting a straight answer from the peddler whether they'd actually watered down the milk. Despite their assurances to the contrary, once we got it home and put it in our tea, it would sometimes become obvious we had been duped.

In a similar way, people today feel the liberty to interpret the Buddha's teachings in their own way. There is an intent to simplify the teachings in order to make them understandable. However, sadly, this "watering down" process can go too far and actually remove the essence of what a teaching may be trying to impart to make it palatable to a wider audience. Yet the Buddhist philosophy on life, happiness, and fulfillment has existed for more than 2,500 years. It is a philosophy of purpose that has worked for millions of people over the millennia. I'm not interested in changing it, nor am I qualified to do so. I have spent forty-five years studying this material, including twelve years in a Tibetan monastery in Nepal, to glean all that I can. In *Six Myths We Live By*, I attempt to present my understanding and learning of some of these vast and profound teachings to you in a way that is accessible, yes, but without changing the meaning.

Chögyam Trungpa Rinpoche, a great pioneer in bringing the Tibetan Buddhist tradition to the modern world, would often say what he was presenting was like "watered-down milk." A good example of watered-down milk is the present trend around self-compassion. My root teacher, Lama Thubten Yeshe, would say, "Be gentle with yourself. If you can be gentle with yourself, you can be gentle with others." But what is the effective way to be gentle or kind to oneself? The self-kindness Lama Yeshe would refer to is a self-kindness that leads to ultimate happiness, not some temporary feel-good state. We need to pay attention to the effects of our self-compassion; we have to be kind but balance that with wisdom. Does your self-care directly work on the causes of your underlying dissatisfaction? To go for a run with the motive of relaxing your body and clearing your mind so you are more effective in helping yourself and others is proper self-compassion. On the other hand, I regularly speak with people who say their "therapy" is exercising. They say they can't be happy without their daily burst of endorphins generated through working out. But this is a limited motivation, focused only on a short-term personal gain. They are not being deeply kind to themselves and others, but rather increasing their dependency on an endorphin hit. Lama Yeshe advocated for forms of self-kindness that are helpful for the long term, as a support for lasting contentment.

What's happened in our culture, because we are so materialistic and self-absorbed, is that self-compassion has become the latest indulgence in increasing "me-ness." That can be destructive in the long term. One of my psychotherapy clients sent her son back to his dad in Florida because she said she needed to work on herself more. Of course, there are many scenarios in which it is more beneficial for a child to be separated from a parent. However, in this case there was no abuse or harm in their relationship, and she clearly stated that she "needed more time for herself." I have empathy for her, and it is of course difficult to judge someone's intentions; still, I saw this particular situation as one that would most likely damage her relationship with her son rather than strengthen their bond. My point here is that we really need to look at the topic of self-compassion and whether it is truly beneficial for oneself and others or just a furthering our self-indulgence. If self-compassion and self-care ultimately lead to one being happier and healthier, and thus more able to be of positive benefit to others, I'm all for it. Self-compassion, like any other Buddhist strategy, is about using each circumstance to improve ourselves so we are better able to have a positive impact. Self-compassion, when used properly, allows one to take care of oneself while not getting hijacked by self-centeredness. Being considerate of others is not the same as being codependent. Codependency is often driven by fear, low self-worth, and strong attachment. Being considerate is looking after others but not at the expense of one's own well-being, especially emotional well-being. It is a balance. When overly focused on our own well-being, we can become strongly me-focused, to the point where we become uncomfortable and ill at ease. We become uptight, anxious, and neurotic. These distinctions are crucial, and they are becoming lost.

You'll want to keep reading this book if you're after the truth of human existence, not another quick fix to feel good. If you've studied Buddhism before, the concepts, references, and connections herein should all check out solidly. Beyond that, I hope this book will be a welcome source of truth to seekers in general. If you are looking for a guide to self-development, if not self-help, or view psychology as a means of development: welcome. Bring your earnestness and curiosity; we'll leave sophisticated metaphysics and mental gymnastics at the door as we shine a light on the myths that have thus far ruled our lives.

The Truth of Suffering

One way to think about our condition, the human condition of suffering, is to substitute the word *problems* for *suffering*. So, we could talk about the first noble truth as the "truth of problems." What this means is that we are constantly set up for problems and have no real protection to keep them from occurring. Problems, in Buddhist psychology and philosophy, are categorized in multiple ways. For example, there are the eight sufferings, the six sufferings, and the three sufferings. Some of these categories just refer to the difficulties humans face, and some apply to all living beings. They each demand a further explanation of their meaning. For example, in the eight sufferings, two of the eight are somewhat related: the suffering of not getting what one wants and the suffering of being separated from people and things one likes.

In conventional thinking, we would not think of these as "suffering." But in Buddhism, suffering is a state of being in which one is never satisfied. And we constantly strive for events, material things, and relationships where we will be satisfied. We want them to last, but they never do. There is always a mindset of wanting more, and yet we can never have everything we want. So the mind becomes disturbed when we put effort into getting what we want and then are unable to succeed or maintain the "buzz." This is pretty much a constant struggle. Obviously, this pattern may be stronger in some people, but nonetheless it regularly upsets our equilibrium. We are always wanting and never fulfilled in any long-lasting sense. We have to ask ourselves, with anything we acquire or achieve, *How long does the glow last, the buzz, the sense of fulfillment?* Typically, we get excited when we think of upgrading our smartphone, and we feel a bit of a buzz when we get it and set it up. Then frustration kicks in when we can't get apps to load or forget our passwords and can't quite set it up like our old one. It's only a short matter of time before it's just an ordinary tool and we are left with not having achieved the (unconscious) satisfaction we sought. The same dynamic happens when we fall in love. The "honeymoon period" is relatively short-lived, and we spend a lot of effort, even in therapy, trying to either recapture the old feelings or find new ones to sustain the warmth we felt when we fell in love in the beginning. And on and on.

The various categories of suffering are not meant to contradict each other, nor are some to be considered more accurate than others. They are articulated differently for the practitioner to connect with or understand how problems—that is, suffering—work. There is no "right" way to understand them, but there are many wrong ways; when we operate from a faulty philosophy on the causes of happiness and suffering, we are continually led astray. We are, for example, told that if one achieves the American Dream, then that is the fulfillment of this life and the achievement of happiness. But it is not the fulfillment of lasting happiness. We attend college so we can get our "dream" job. Such achievements, while important for a secure life, do little in the achievement of lasting happiness and can, in fact, be more conditions for the pattern of dissatisfaction, problems, and suffering to continue. So we can understand that these categories of suffering are just different ways for each individual to get a sense of our human condition and its dissatisfactoriness or problemness—two words I just made up for this occasion.

So the Buddha presented many ways to help us come to terms with the predicament living beings face: the truth of suffering, the eight sufferings, the six sufferings, the three sufferings. These are all explanations that try to convince us that our existence is problematic. Of course, our existence is not *only* problematic, for we also possess the key to liberation and lasting fulfillment. But as we live our lives now, and have forever in the past, we have existed in the prison of problems—without even knowing we are in prison. One then has to wonder whether ignorance is bliss: "If I don't know I'm in prison, then is it so bad?" Anyone who sees the prison that ignorance is, however, in juxtaposition to freedom, would never feel that prison is a better option. It is vital to understand, therefore, that the Buddha's method is founded in this understanding: psychologically speaking, we will never seek liberation, which is the ultimate well-being, without first accepting that life is hugely problematic and then understanding the causes of those problems. Then, in addition, we need a solid belief in the fact that there is a better way to live. This "better way to live" is put in the context that we exist forever by reincarnating over and over and over again. So while the journey and work to attain liberation may include some temporary hardships, these hardships are nothing when compared to the eternal hardships we endure when sticking with the idea that "ignorance is bliss."

Some of the sufferings or problems the Buddha wants us to confront are things like the problem of loneliness, the problem of dying, the problem with sickness, the problem with aging, the problem of never being satisfied, the problems that arise when we don't get what we want and then, on the other hand, when we get what we don't want—and even when we get what we want, we eventually lose it or our happiness eventually fades. These conditions haunt us endlessly. And while it may seem like these conditions don't really last, they do repeat themselves over and over and over and over again, ad infinitum. This is what is meant by the truth of suffering.

Why Myths?

There are many ways we try to escape the truth of suffering. In this book, I will take up six of them—what I am calling "myths." While these myths that we believe may seem to soften the blows of life, they in fact only perpetuate our problems. Why have I chosen the word *myth*? Myth is another way of saying "inaccurate view." You could contrast a myth, then, with a fact, like the fact that the earth is round. When you don't see that the earth is round or believe others who tell you that it is, then you believe the earth is flat. Your belief in that myth does something for you. It provides you comfort even as your ignorance of the fact that the earth is round persists.

The six myths I have chosen to present here inhabit our consciousness twenty-four hours a day, and have done so since the beginning of time—that is, if we believe in reincarnation. If you don't believe in reincarnation, they have still haunted us since the beginning of this life. Just because you believe in a myth, however, doesn't mean it is true. For example, one of the myths we will be exploring in this book is the myth of randomness. The opposite of this myth is karma, one of the basic laws promoted through Buddhist thought. For Buddhists, people who don't accept or "believe in" karma seem strange, the same way we might consider the views of a flat-earther to be strange—a lack of acceptance of basic science.

Calm Abiding

To come to an understanding that the earth is, in fact, round, we might go to space—an expensive and unlikely proposition. You might observe how lunar eclipses show the earth's circular shadow or read about those ships that have circumnavigated the globe. To penetrate to the heart of any of the six myths we live by, however, we need only go inside, further and further, through the practice of meditation to the state known as "calm abiding."

The technical definition of calm abiding, or *shamatha*, as it is known in Sanskrit, is a state of serenity accompanied by physical and mental pliancy and their simultaneous forms of bliss. That's a bit of a wordy explanation, but it helps to have the exact definition in order to properly unpack the concept and use it correctly. Today in Western societies, as I've mentioned, concepts surrounding meditation, mindfulness, mental relaxation, concentrated attention, and so on, are prevalent without being very specific. Various forms of meditation have proliferated: music meditation, nature meditation, breath meditation, movement meditation, transcendental meditation, and so on.

Here, in the Buddhist context, we mean something very specific by *shamatha* meditation. First, meditation is a tool, not a goal. The goal is calm abiding. When engaging in the development of calm abiding, the meditator, or practitioner, traverses through several preliminary stages before actually attaining the state of calm abiding. The attainment of calm abiding is measured when the meditator can stay on his or her object of meditation without wavering or distraction, without becoming foggy or sleepy or excited, for as long as they want to stay in that concentrated state. Objects include the breath, a visualization, a concept, or an external aid like particular figures or objects that produce a positive effect. In beginning stages of developing calm abiding the statute of the Buddha, for example, is used. It is said that when one can stay one-pointedly on the object of meditation for four hours without wavering, then one can be said to have attained single-pointed concentration. Calm abiding can then be attained, which is a state of mind beyond single-pointed concentration. When the meditator reaches this state, it is accompanied by the attainment of physical and mental pliancy, or bliss—this is the true sign one has achieved calm abiding. Furthermore, it must be understood that the state of calm abiding is a state of clarity and stability. There are other various meditative states where clarity can be achieved without stability, and stability can be attained without clarity. These are not calm abiding, though they may be quite exalted states of mind. Without clarity and stability, we cannot then purely generate the necessary insights and realizations that we wish to attain in our path to complete freedom.

This may seem like a tall order for those of us just starting out on the path. I present what the end of the path looks like here as an aspirational goal, but we can begin just where we are by generating the realization, the insight, that there are, in fact, myths we live by. Every myth spoken about here is the opposite of a piece of reality. To overcome these beginningless myths that infect our mind, we must first generate the insight into the truths that these myths obscure—and it is my hope that this book helps you to do that. In order to hold or maintain those insights, to fully integrate those aha moments—that is where meditation comes in. In part 2 of the book, I have placed six meditation practices that are designed to help you realize the truth behind each of the six myths in turn. I often call these "time-ins," a linguistic trick to emphasize that this is time to go inward. A *time-out* is typically meant as a time to withdraw physically from a difficult situation and seek some space. Here, we are also seeking space, but inner space. It is not a time to check out but to check in. It is a combination of realization and meditation that will fully transform myths and their accompanying support system or "scaffolding" into happiness and freedom. As of now, we are still wobbly; our peace is fragile. We all have probably had, for example, some insight into death and its profundity. An aha about death or impermanence might lead to a direct experience of the beauty of this precious life of ours. But because we do not have calm abiding, or even strong concentration, we are unable to fully use these insights to travel the path of eternal freedom from pain, suffering, disappointment, and depression. The attainment of calm abiding is the solution.

To anticipate your experience of the practices in part 2 of this book, I will say a few things here. First, calm abiding is not just a practice in mindfulness, at least not in the commonly understood sense of the practice. To equate mindfulness and calm abiding is like saying miniature golf is golf. Of course, there are some common features, but if you've only ever played miniature golf, those skills won't help you play even one hole on a real golf course.

The development of calm abiding is a detailed process that takes time. One needs to train just like training for a marathon. There are many key elements in training for a race of 26.2 miles. Just developing one's leg strength, for example, is not adequate. The practices, or "time-ins," at the end of this book will get you started in your training. No real internal change can happen by merely reading a book, watching a YouTube video, or listening to a podcast. Internal change can only happen through internal practices. Watching a fitness video will never get you in shape if you don't climb on the treadmill and actively train your muscles. It has been researched that real internal change can come about by just meditating fifteen minutes a day for two weeks.

The Teachings Should Sell Themselves

I don't want to try to convince you of the value of calm abiding or the methods that can be used to approach that state with increasing skill and vigor. This book is only an invitation to you to explore the value of calm abiding for yourself. There is a well-known quote from the Buddha, who said, "Do not accept my ideas out of respect for me. No. You should put them to the test as a metalsmith will test the authenticity of gold. The goldsmith will burn it, rub it, hammer it, and then will make a judgment on its authenticity and purity. Likewise, put my teachings to the same examination."

When I heard my very first teaching from Lama Zopa Rinpoche, I was in a state of shock when he repeated this quote from Shakyamuni Buddha. I couldn't believe that I was being given permission to question, to doubt, to investigate. Not only was I being given permission, but I was being encouraged to! Prior to that, all of my spiritual mentors outside of Buddhism had encouraged me to accept on faith what they taught.

Not long after hearing this teaching, I returned to the United States from Nepal, where I had secured a coveted internship. It would require a one-hour commute, and for that I would need a better car than the one I owned. I went to look at a used car in San Jose, about forty minutes from my home in Santa Cruz, California. I had the classified ads laid out on the passenger seat along with my Thomas Guide road maps book—no GPS back then. I was going to look at a used Mazda sedan. Interestingly, since the ads were listed alphabetically, I notice just above the *M*s were the *L*s . . . and my eye fell upon an ad for a used Lexus. I was not really looking for a Lexus since I knew they'd be way out of my price range. They'd only hit the market a few years earlier, and being a luxury car, I did not even entertain the idea of being able to purchase one. And yet, there one was, and within my price range. Essentially, the ad was just a teaser to get people to come to the lot in search of this great deal only to find out it had "just been sold, but would you be interested in another model?" (For more money, of course!) It just so happened that this was the first day this car was listed. I decided to swing by the lot on the way to checking out the Mazda.

When I pulled into the Lexus dealership, I was pretty intimidated. I didn't belong here. But now it got quite interesting. My hackles were up waiting to defend myself against an aggressive used-car salesman. What I found instead was a polite, low-key guy who asked if he could help me with something.

I told him about the ad, to which he replied, "Would you like to test-drive it?"

I said, "Sure. But just to let you know, I'm certain it's out of my price range."

"Don't worry. No obligations. It's just that they're fun to drive. Let's go."

So I took the five-speed manual for a test drive. He told me to get on the freeway so I can "see what this car can do." He made sure I got up into fifth gear. Then, down the freeway, he told me to take a particular exit with a nice curving off-ramp so I could see how well the car cornered. We were back in the sales lot twenty minutes later. He got out and nonchalantly said to me, "If you need anything else, I'll be in my office."

Huh? I stood out in the lot for some minutes pondering my options. I finally went in and asked him if he could budge on the price. He said he couldn't really, since it was so low already. But I was sold. I bought it and, in the end, I asked him, "So what's the deal?"

"What do you mean?" he politely asked.

I said, "How come you never came at me with the hard sell?"

"Oh! We don't need to do that. The car sells itself. We just organize the paperwork."

In a similar way, Buddhist teachings should sell themselves. As His Holiness the Dalai Lama says, if one finds something too difficult to accept at the moment, then just put it to the side and maybe revisit it in the future. In the practice of contemplation, our job is to look at all the angles so that we fully understand, at least intellectually, the topic at hand. In Buddhist psychology there are two kinds of doubt: healthy doubt and afflicted doubt. Healthy doubt is when you doubt a teaching but are open to the fact that it could be true. For example, the teachings on karma—that is, cause and effect—are subtle and challenging, and we should question them. But such questioning is best when it is situated in the context of thinking that something could be true, but you just don't get it right now—and you continue to investigate. Unhealthy doubt is the doubt similar to what the professional skeptic feels—you may know someone like this—they think it is their job to debunk everything and not actually search for the truth, if the truth is contradictory to their belief.

No Quick Fixes

One of the challenges you might come up against as you read this book is wanting an immediate insight into life beyond myths, or some flash of wisdom that will immediately fix all your problems. But as tempting as it is to seek out a quick fix, I urge you to put in the effort and let yourself work with these myths thoroughly and deeply. Years ago, I was fortunate to attend a teaching by the Dalai Lama on *bodhichitta*, the altruistic aspiration to attain enlightenment for the benefit of all living beings. But one of the most profound takeaways from these teachings was about our desire for the quick fix. He told a story of Milarepa, who is perhaps Tibet's most famous and adored Buddhist saint, and of one of his disciples, Gampopa. Prior to becoming a student of Milarepa, Gampopa was a doctor. He then lived and studied under Milarepa for some years, becoming one of the heirs to Milarepa's teachings. At one point, when Milarepa saw that Gampopa had received all that he had to offer, Milarepa conveyed to Gampopa that the time had come for him to go out on his own and spread the teachings he'd received from his master. Milarepa instructed him to prepare for his departure, and then when the time came to depart in a few days, Milarepa explained that as a sign of respect for his disciple, he would escort him for the first few miles of his journey. At this point in the story, His Holiness had tears streaming down his face, as if he himself were experiencing this event that happened nearly a thousand years earlier.

Still teary, His Holiness went on to relate how when the day arrived, and Milarepa and Gampopa came to a bridge a few miles down the road, Milarepa stated that it was now time for Gampopa to continue alone on his journey. As Gampopa climbed a hill after crossing the bridge, he had a kind of panic attack. He thought, *Maybe I didn't get all of my master's teachings. Maybe there is something still remaining to receive from him.* He turned around and saw his guru off in the distance and shouted out, "Dear Master, are you sure I received your entire lineage of teachings? Isn't there something still I need to receive?"

Milarepa assured him that he had received the entire lineage of both his outer and inner teachings. In Buddhism, the "outer" teachings are considered all of the scriptures, commentaries, teachings, and so on. In other words, they are those teachings that are educational and meant for study. The "inner" teachings are those that are the actualization of those outer teachings. This is achieved primarily through meditation practices, of which there are thousands of variations, and is an internal experience that transforms one's present mental habits into healthier, deeper, and more insightful attitudes and perceptions. Realizing the nature of the mind, and then actualizing its potential, can only occur through an internal process. Additionally, in the Buddhist tradition, and especially the Tibetan Vajrayana tradition, the role of an outer *guru*, or teacher, is paramount in the student's actualization of these deep internal practices. The outer teacher becomes a role model that becomes internalized for the adept.

Gampopa still had some uncertainty, however, so he asked, "Master, of all the teachings you've imparted to me, please tell me, what is the most important teaching you gave me? What is the teaching that is supreme of all your teachings?"

His Holiness again had to pause in his relating of this story. Milarepa, in response to his student's heartfelt query, turned his back to his disciple and raised the threadbare cloth he wore to show his buttocks, exposing the callouses that had formed over years of meditating in cold, hard caves. Then he said, "*This* is my most important teaching! Practice!" Milarepa then continued on his way without another word or glance back.

There was complete silence in the auditorium as His Holiness buried his face in his upper robe, wiping his tears. After the immediate emotion had passed, His Holiness commented, "I'm feeling more and more comfortable with the idea of taking three eons to become enlightened."

As you engage in the difficult task of uncovering and overcoming the myths you have been living by, my hope is that you too have this same patience and determination. In my own habitual thinking, I find myself constantly up against the challenge of being patient. I think a primary goal of our modern culture, particularly with the advent of the technology revolution, is that we expect to achieve everything more quickly and easily, with minimal effort. The spiritual path, in my belief, will never be able to imitate or duplicate that approach. While there will most certainly be scientific and technological breakthroughs that will assist people in developing more awareness, calmness, and deeper knowledge into the workings of the mind and emotions, the actual work of transforming the mind will be mostly left up to age-old, tried and tested, ancient interventions. These interventions worked for people 2,500 years ago. And people a thousand years after that. And, again, people a thousand years after that—and up to the present day. They have worked in cultures and civilizations that have been distinct and different from each other, and there is no real reason to think we are that much different. Of course, I'm referring here not to the cultural manifestations of Buddhism in these disparate societies but the universal aspect of the Buddha's teachings. The Buddha's teachings are beyond culture and religion. That is why they are universal.

Part 1

The Myths

1
The Myth of Reality

The myth of reality is the fundamental myth we live by—the granddaddy of them all. We mistakenly see the world—and ourselves—as a result of this fundamental misperception of reality. Reality here is both a philosophical topic and a day-to-day topic. In this discussion we are only really interested in how the philosophical theory impacts our everyday life. Simply put, the definition of *reality* is that things appear in the way they exist. Buddhist theory posits that since we actually do not see things the way they truly exist, then we are in constant relationship—actions and reactions—with things as we incorrectly perceive them. Thus, the conclusion can be made that if we are responding to things, people, events, even ourselves, in the way they do not exist, then this has consequences. And those consequences work against our lasting happiness and peace—the goal of our life. On the flip side, having a clear understanding of how our mind works is the foundation to understanding reality, and understanding reality is the key to mental health and well-being. So we can say that not having a correct perception or experience of reality is the root of every living being's discontent, confusion, and conflict.

All subsequent myths, and one might say all of Buddhist thought and practice, flow from the myth of reality. It is the foundation for the entire psychological and spiritual development of the adept. It is said that Shakyamuni Buddha taught his entire corpus of teachings, over one hundred volumes, for the sole purpose of leading beings into an understanding of reality. It is the very breath of the living body of Buddhism.

So Why Talk about Anything Else?

Having stressed the importance of the understanding of the nature of reality, one could ask, "So what's up with the other 84,000 things the Buddha taught and all those practices we're supposed to engage with? What about those instructions in meditation, teachings on developing compassion and the laws of cause and effect, and the rest? Why didn't the Buddha just teach this key topic and cut to the chase?"

I received my answer to this question when I was living at Kopan Monastery in Nepal. One of my duties there was to manage the annual month-long "November Course." In those days, in the mid-1970s, it was not easy for a Westerner to study teachings in Tibetan Buddhism because very little had been translated. There were very few qualified translators, let alone lamas who spoke English. But the founders of Kopan, Lama Thubten Yeshe and Lama Zopa Rinpoche, were unique in that they did speak English (albeit a sort of unique dialect that was learned from their hippie students), and at the request of their students, they would regularly offer teachings on the various topics of Tibetan Buddhism.

The November Course was an immersive experience that involved many hours of instruction by the lamas accompanied by many hours of meditation. In the second half of the course, participants took precepts, observed silence, and ate just a single meal each day. It was intense, to say the least. It was meant to be strict in order to foster a sense of retreat from one's ordinary life.

One day, I went to see Lama Yeshe with a concern. Some students were sneaking out of the facilities to go down the hill to get better food, a shower, and maybe smoke a cigarette or get high. These things were of course strictly forbidden during the one-month course. Feeling indignant about their behavior, I asked what I should do to try to corral these few rule-breakers and bring them back in line. As I voiced my complaints, I was sure I had a sympathetic ear with Lama Yeshe. But as was often the case during my nine years under his guidance, I was set straight. Lama simply looked at me and said, "People are at different levels, dear."

The Buddha did not only teach about the nature of reality, but instead taught 84,000 different teachings because, similarly, "people are at different levels." While understanding the nature of reality is core to breaking our misperceptions and finding a path out of suffering, people are of such different places in their development. The skillfulness of the Buddhist approach is that while the development of the insight into reality is the core practice for becoming liberated from our problems, getting to this insight is a long and gradual process. If, for example, someone is overwhelmed by distractions, as in truth all us are, then we need to attend to these distractions first so that our mind can develop at least some ability to focus on reality itself. Working on distractions like desire, attachment, irritability, anxiety, and so on can take years to get a handle on. This why there are so many methods and interventions in Buddhist therapeutic practice. Compassion is the primary attitude that assists the awakening to reality. Many of us need a great deal of work on developing compassion. The compassion referred to in Buddhist practice, the compassion that aids the awakening of wisdom—the view of reality—is a compassion that extends to all living beings, especially the people we don't like or feel justified in despising.

On a related note, His Holiness the Dalai Lama often observes how wonderful it is to have different religions and spiritual paths in the world so that there can be a system of spiritual improvement for many different kinds of people. People have such various dispositions that it is unreasonable that any one method, theory, or religion can speak to all people's needs.

What Do We Mean by Reality?

One aspect about Buddhist teachings that I deeply appreciate is that terms need to be defined before one can have a conversation about them. We all speak about *love*, for instance—but what is love? When we tell someone we love them, is that the same love as when we say we love a pair of shoes? Is loving a beautiful sunset the same as loving our dog? I was watching a reality show the other night, and when one of the contestants got voted off by his competitors, he gave them hugs and as he was leaving, said, "Love you guys!" Surely that isn't the same love as I have for my mother! To have a dialogue about love, we have to be on the same page about what it means. The definition of *love* in Buddhist philosophy is actually quite simple: Love is the wish and attitude that another being experiences happiness, and the act of loving that being is the not just the attitude to wish them happiness but to ensure their happiness, even at the expense of one's own. It is not a contrived practice, but a spontaneous and natural one that is developed first by working on it with some level of manufactured love, whether through design or fabrication. Genuine love is not so hard to understand when reflecting on a mother's authentic and spontaneous love for her child. She doesn't think about feeling empathy when her baby cries. It's natural and spontaneous. This is a similar kind of love, though absent of an emotional attachment, and can be developed for all living beings. With this kind of mental development, along with the development of other healthy attitudes like compassion, equanimity, and nonviolence, the development of wisdom, the wisdom of reality, comes easily. Just a side note: As one develops these healthy mental states, wisdom deepens. As wisdom deepens, so do these other wonderful attitudes. Thus, they can be considered codependent. As the well-known Buddhist saying goes, "Wisdom without compassion, and vice versa, is like a bird trying to fly with one wing."

For our conversation about reality, the way the term will be employed here is to mean "that which exists in the way it appears." In other words, for it to be "reality," the way we perceive something—whether with our eyes, the other four senses, or our mind—has to appear to us in the exact same way it exists. There is an implication here that if it exists the way it appears, then it must appear that exact same way to everyone else, at least everyone with functioning senses and a healthy mind. Seems pretty straightforward, right?

During those many years I lived in Nepal, my father would get frustrated that I was not interested in returning to live in the United States. He would say to me, "When are you going to come back and live in the real world?" This statement was always curious to me. I would reflect on the fact that I was living in one of the poorest countries in the world, where walking down the street I would see people, some of them beggars, with diseases I'd only ever read about. I encountered people with leprosy, with tumors on their heads or faces the size of grapefruits, with elephantiasis, with scars from smallpox, and with limbs that were merely broken but with inadequate health care could not be reset properly. Funeral processions would weave their way down the narrow streets of the bazaar with crying family and friends in tow. At the same time, there might be a mother watching the procession while she oiled and massaged her newborn. Feral dogs roamed among the vegetable and fruit sellers displaying their goods in vibrant colors next to the butcher store, which had the head of a water buffalo hanging outside the shop, displaying the shop's goods as if it were a neon sign. The streets were dusty and dirty, but at the same time sweet incense would waft through the crowded alleyways, leading to hidden shrines and temples that might be hundreds if not thousands of years old. Here, a family having had a poor harvest would be supported by the other villagers; despite the poverty of the area, starvation was rare. And once, when I had taken a Tibetan friend to the hospital, we sat in shock as we overheard a doctor explain to a nearby patient that he had contracted rabies from a dog bite, and it was too late for the treatment to be effective. This young French couple had just come back to town from a trek in the Himalayas; evidently the gentleman had been bitten by a dog in a remote village some three or four days earlier. Now he was going to die of rabies.

Given that I bore witness to such life and death and disease every day, when my dad would make this comment, "When are you going to come back to the real world?" I would think, *Well, Dad, this place seems pretty darn real to me.* I would reflect on the fact that in Los Angeles, where I grew up, I would never see beggars on the street (this was before the homelessness crisis we now face). In fact, for me and my friends, our feet almost never touched the concrete. We'd go to the perfect beach to surf waves in an ocean straight from a fantasy while the majority of the world was looking for food. Our lives seemed straight out of Hollywood, which was just around the corner creating fantasy worlds for the silver screen and TV. We went to work to earn enough money so we could party on the weekend with our choice of drugs to "escape reality," and yet this was considered normal "real" life. It seemed our goal was—for most of us, is—to weed out all the unpleasantness of life and increase the pleasurable aspects that feel good. But reality is more about coming to the realization that things in life are actually difficult, painful, and dissatisfying, and that our pursuit to numb this pain through pleasure seems, well, pretty unreal, and unrealistic.

Perception Is Not Reality

When David Copperfield, the renowned illusionist, makes the Statue of Liberty disappear before an audience of thousands of people, we somehow know that is not real. It looks like the monument disappears—our eyes don't perceive it anymore—but our rational mind tells us it can't be so. We know, somehow, that the appearance—or in this case, the lack of appearance—of the Statue of Liberty is not the way it actually exists. So we say, "That's not real." People would think we were nuts if we were to start protesting to David Copperfield that he has destroyed the statue and threaten to file a lawsuit against him if he doesn't return it. The audience accepts that the Statue of Liberty didn't *actually* disappear. They accept it is merely an illusion.

On the other hand, we've all been scared by things we're sure are there—we think someone is trying to break into our house after we hear a scratching sound on a window; we glimpse a man lurking in the shadows; or we develop a sense of paranoia when we think we overhear someone talking about us. Only, instead we find there's a breeze blowing a branch on our window, a bush in the shadows of the night, or two people are talking about the player who struck out at last night's baseball game and not us.

If we react to these false perceptions as if they are real, we create distress and act in a way that is not only unnecessary but disturbing and emotionally jarring to ourselves and others. We might call the police because we are scared someone is breaking into our house. We might start an argument with the two people who we think are talking about us behind our backs.

Of course, these examples are relatively minor, but it gets worse—much worse. There have been countless murders, for example, that have occurred due to misperception. But I want to draw your attention to one particular case that highlights the devastating consequences of racial prejudice that obscures correct perception.

Ahmaud Arbery was gunned down by three men as he ran through their neighborhood. The three white men saw Mr. Arbery, an African American man, as a burglar running from the scene of a crime. However, Mr. Arbery was only a jogger out for a run, something he did frequently. The jury found the three men guilty of murder and committing a hate crime. These three men's misperception of reality had horrific consequences. "Reality" is actually conditional, and in this case, mistaken interpretations of reality were deadly and catastrophic for all parties involved.

Here's my point, and it's an old one: Perception is not reality. If something, be it an object, an experience, a belief, and so on, exists in such a way that it appears differently for different people because it is dependent upon conditions, then that perception cannot be real. To be real, everyone would have to perceive it the same way, because that's the way the object, experience, or belief exists. Reality, by definition, means it maintains its true nature in all conditions and at all times. If it changes for each person, each perceiver, then it is not real. It is something else.

On a far lighter note than the tragic story related above, allow me to recall a story about three umpires having a beer after a baseball game. One umpire says to the others, "There's balls and there's strikes, and I call them as they are." The second umpire, seeking to correct the first umpire, says, "Well, actually, there are balls and strikes, and I call them as I see them." The third umpire, quietly listening to the discussion, chimes in and says, "Well, sorry, guys, you are both wrong. There are balls and strikes, and they're nothing until I call them!"

This captures the central Buddhist idea of how we create our own reality—which, then, cannot be called reality at all. As the French American diarist Anaïs Nin said, "We see things not as they are, but as we are. Because it is the 'I' behind the 'eye' that does the seeing." There may be no better quote among modern writers to illustrate the main point I am making here. When the various Buddhist philosophical schools debate the nature of reality, they argue about a central question: "How exactly do things exist?" Our natural notion, the one we go through life with, is that things exist "out there," on their own, independent, really, truly, concretely, inherently. But when we delve into the deepest philosophical questions, we discover a different way of explaining, and locating, reality.

Transference in Therapy

That we create our own reality was something that modern psychology caught on to on a rudimentary level pretty early on. Sigmund Freud's theory of transference is a central concept in psychotherapy, or psychoanalysis, as it was referred to in his time. Freud identified transference as something that occurred in the therapeutic context. Initially, it was considered pathological. Later theorists expanded the understanding of this mechanism to include other close or intimate relationships and posited that it could be seen as either beneficial or harmful.

In brief, transference in therapy is the act of the client unknowingly transferring feelings about someone from their past onto the therapist. Transference could then be analyzed in order to account for distortions in a client's perceptions of reality. Transference is a multilayered and complex event that happens when the brain tries to understand a current experience by examining it through the past. However, in Buddhist psychology, this process of past experience coloring our present experience happens essentially all the time. In other words, expanding the concept of transference, we can say that we are pretty much engaged in transference at every moment, though at very different levels of subtlety or concreteness.

Transference is not a word psychologists use much anymore, preferring the more modern term *projection*. Both involve redirecting feelings from past relationships onto a current relationship, specifically attributing one's own thoughts, feelings, or behaviors to someone else. If we leave transference to the interrelationship with a therapist and use projection to describe, say, the experience of being in a couple, then it becomes pretty evident in couples counseling that there is a lot of projection going on.

A partner might complain about the other partner in almost the exact terms they would, and have, used toward their mother or father or even a previous boyfriend or girlfriend. They do this often without realizing it. In the same way, when we meet people with whom we just immediately sync with or dislike, we don't realize until later it was because they reminded us of someone else. People who have been traumatized, particularly due to physical or sexual abuse, have a difficult time not projecting those past events onto present ones. A person may remind them of their abuser, and this makes it difficult to have an authentic relationship. Buddhist psychology tells us that we very rarely, if ever, see things as they really are. In fact, we are always projecting qualities onto people and objects alike. In romantic relationships there is so much projection going on, with such exaggerated qualities being ascribed to one's lover, it can seem almost hallucinatory to an outside observer.

Let me give you an example from my psychotherapy practice (names and identifying details have been changed in order to protect confidentiality). James was a fifty-two-year-old single man with two adult children. He was the type of guy who "loved women" (his words) and loved being in relationships with them. He ran a successful veterinary practice, though much of the proceeds went to support his two ex-wives. He was head over heels about his latest relationship with Alana, a Serbian woman ten years younger than he was. Alana was attractive and had also been married before. She described her previous marriage as physically abusive, but said James was perfect because he was "gentle and kind." James was also financially secure and owned his own home and some acreage. Alana was visiting on a tourist visa—a red flag for me, but I did not want to be overly suspicious and was willing to have couples counseling with an open mind.

Something felt a bit off from the beginning of my sessions with them. What I mean by "off" is it seemed something important was not being verbalized or was being kept hidden. This is not unusual in therapy. Of course, if you're a psychotherapist who helps others with their emotional, relationship, and psychological problems, then you expect the unexpected. That's the nature of the job. Otherwise, it's like a firefighter going out on a call and being surprised to smell smoke.

James would fawn over Alana in our sessions, speak consistently about her beauty and qualities, her spirituality, his love for her. Alana would speak of James's kindness and ability to provide a good home. He was security, she said. Our sessions did not go on for a long time as they mainly were coming in to validate their relationship to each other with me as their witness. Eventually they got married, despite most of his friends trying to talk him out of it. He couldn't see he was projecting his own needs for companionship, fear of being alone, and insecurity on to his relationship with Alana. Everyone else could perceive his projections except him. That is usually the case.

About two years later James called me. He wanted to come in on his own. Alana and he were breaking up. After securing a green card, she was now demanding financial support. She claimed to own half of his property, and he was now faced with having to sell his beloved home.

The Buddhist Take on Projection

So who were James and Alana, really? One can see that they each projected their own needs upon the other person. This is the kind of projection that is familiar to most people. Within the Buddhist context, however, the concept of projection goes much further and deeper to what we might call a "double projection." It's a projection on top of a projection.

As one of my teachers, Geshe Gelek, often says, "We see what isn't there and we don't see what is there." He is telling us that we superimpose and exaggerate qualities onto an object that are pure fabrications. Something fabricated can't hold the label of being "real"—fabricated and real are mutually exclusive terms. To be clear, when we discuss that we do not experience or perceive things as they really are, we are not saying they don't exist at all. In Buddhist thought there is *conventional reality*, a reality that is established by agreement and shared perception and the function of whatever thing we are referring to in particular. We say that conventional reality is *valid,* the coffee mug on the table is not a clock because it functions as a mug, but the way we perceive the *true nature* of the mug is erroneous. So while we say that what we perceive conventionally is valid, it is still perceived erroneously with respect to its actual nature.

What we are saying is things don't exist in the way we are experiencing them. When we see a coiled hose as a snake, that snake does not exist; it is still, on some level, a coiled hose. But that hose does not exist "out there," either, as an independently existing hose. There is a hose that functions to deliver water, but we never see or experience the *real* hose or the real person or the real world that my father wanted me to return to.

This is what I mean by a double projection. Not only do we not see the true nature of what we perceive, we also project a nature or a reality on top of the thing we perceive. I think that matters when we begin to look at it that way. What matters is that not only when we see, or perceive, something we immediately see it "not as it is," but then on top of that bare perception, we then elaborate with all kinds of assumptions, projections, and further observations. So we think we perceive our experience correctly, and then further believe in all the embellishments we ascribe to that experience. It's like a double false misinterpretation. By *perception*, what is meant is any experience of the five senses: eye (sights), ear (sounds), nose (smells), tongue (tastes), or body (tactile sensations). Additionally, we say that the mind also has a sense, since it perceives thoughts, images, dreams, and so on. But the mind's sense power is not physical, like the rest. Each of these sense experiences, all of the time, are perceived in ways that do not actually exist.

Why is that so important to understand? Because suffering in Buddhism is not about pain only. It is at least as much about confusion and ignorance. Here, *confusion* refers to the fact that we do not see reality, not even for a single instant, in our entire life. Exploring suffering is important because it gets us to realize the things with which we are constantly in relationship—objects, people, thoughts, emotions, even ourselves—don't exist the way we perceive them . . . *at all.*

Traditional sources often explain that we are constantly hallucinating our world, our experience, as if it is like a dream. That means we're never touching the essence of life—we are always in relationship with a fantasy we've created, and we not only don't know this, we actually firmly believe that what we see really exists, just as it appears. There are just two things we are hallucinating: our sense of self or identity or personality (as we will explore in the next chapter) and, then, the entire external world that is entirely engaged with through our five senses as well as our mind. It's as if we're in relationship with a hologram, and we call that hologram our wife/husband/partner and believe we're relating with something real and solid when, in fact, it's nothing but a projection. So we fight with this hologram. We make love with this hologram. We go to war for this hologram and fight against other holograms. We yell at holograms in their hologram cars for driving stupidly. Of course, a hologram or an illusion or a hallucination or a dream is not *exactly* the same as a person or phenomena. But the way we experience them is similar. And this way of thinking is often recommended by Buddhist teachers as a way for us to wake up to the fact that what we see and experience is not real, but some form of projection. "Awaken," remember, is the translation of the word *buddha*. All of these philosophical ideas are actually *experienced* when one develops a mind that is sharpened through the practice of meditation. Then, these philosophical and psychological ideas become experiences—valid experiences.

Celluloid Heroes

In some of the examples we discussed earlier, whether David Copperfield or Ahmaud Arbery, we saw that the perception of an individual creates the prism or conditions through which something is taken to be real. In truth, everything we experience is conditional, but we think it exists exactly as we see it. Our life then is much more akin to a movie than it is to "reality." Movies are illusions that appear as real. They appear as a flowing movement, a stream of images without any space or break between them. In fact, filmmakers have discovered they only need to project twenty-four frames per second to give the illusion of a constant flow of perception when, in fact, it is really simply a series of fast-moving slides.

There are many, many levels of misperception of reality, just like this example of film. These are the myths we live by. While everything is in the nature of movement, we see things as frozen. Reality is a constant flow of images, experiences, feelings, sensations, reactions, and so on, but we only perceive a frozen image before we move on to the next frozen image. This is not in accord with reality, and yet we totally believe it.

The first step is to know that we are watching a movie, something that is a mere construction of interdependent parts and causes. That is extremely powerful and life-changing knowledge. This conceptual perspective starts as an intellectual process, but through reflection and meditation, a correct understanding of reality can be cultivated. At first, this direct perception of reality will be mixed, at varying levels, with conception. When a practitioner begins to cultivate a conceptual experience of reality mixed with a bit of nonconceptual perception, it is at that time that one is considered to have actually entered the path to full awakening. As the conceptions become less solid, one is led to a nonconceptual, direct perception of reality. Such direct perception is beyond words because it is beyond concept. This is the actual spiritual path to awakening. When a person has the direct nonconceptual insight into reality, they never, ever, not for one instant, can regress into the realms of confusion. They are now an awakened being, but more properly, we should say an "awakening" being. This is because the person is not fully awakened, not a complete buddha. The process of full awakening, as we have seen, can now take billions of years or a single lifetime. But one thing is for sure, the awakening being is no longer, nor ever will be, an ordinary being subject to negative states of mind—even as there is still a process that needs to be undertaken where the past negative mind-states need to be purified or dissolved from their mindstream.

Direct Insight into Reality

Can we ever see what isn't there, what lies between the gaps of the movie slides? That's a good question to ask ourselves, and one that is rather deep. Different philosophical schools get into extensive discussions about this very question. These gaps are like space. Can you see space? Or can you only infer what is filling the space?

There are those in the Buddhist tradition, and most likely outside the tradition as well, who have had a direct insight into reality. This direct insight is what the Buddhist practitioner is seeking. Once a person has this direct insight, their life is permanently changed. In the Zen Buddhist tradition this experience is called *satori*. In other Buddhist traditions it is referred to as the insight into emptiness, or suchness, or thusness. We'll talk about the details of this experience later. But at this stage I want to make it clear that this experience is not nirvana or the final attainment of awakening or enlightenment. It is just the beginning of the process of becoming fully liberated, enlightened, free.

Over the millennia, thousands upon thousands of individuals who have pursued the spiritual path, the path of awakening to one's highest potential, have had this insight into reality. From the Buddhist master's perspective, while this experience is life-altering, it is not the place to stop. And yet many do, having thought they have now attained liberation from the world of problems and suffering. This is a big mistake.

When we speak of such an experience as direct insight into reality, we are speaking about an event that has many levels of depth. It does not happen randomly; rather, various causes and conditions allow the experience to arise. The spiritual path, in Buddhism at least, is a structured, calculated methodology that allows this experience of reality to occur. It does not come through prayer, asceticism, or study, although each of these may contribute at different stages. It cannot happen through reading a book or listening to a lecture. It can only really happen in direct experience, typically in meditation.

We all know what it takes to train for a marathon. If we are longtime couch potatoes who never do more exercise than walking from the car to the grocery store, it would be unreasonable to think we could run a marathon after a few weeks of training or less—by simply having the wish to do so. It takes a lot of hard work to get in shape. It takes training because we have habituated ourselves to be a "non-marathon-runner," the antithesis of a marathon runner.

The same is true for developing insight into reality. In fact, the challenge is much more daunting than training to run a marathon. In terms of effort, they are not really comparable. Theoretically, one might be able to run a marathon, or the equivalent for our age, after training for perhaps a year. But according to Buddhist thought, we have had countless previous lifetimes to train the mind and have not really made much progress. We have actually trained our mind to see the *opposite* of reality. Through all of our incarnations, while having varied and different personalities, we have had the same mind. So all the habits we have generated for countless incarnations, similar to the creation of the neuropathways of this life, are embedded in our minds. We have become habituated, day after day, year after year, and lifetime after lifetime, to see unreality.

It is a massively strenuous effort to overcome this false perception, but it is worth it. When we fully understand and accept that an afflicted mind, a mind adhering to the disturbing emotions, is a mind that creates unhappiness, discontent, and imbalance, then we can begin to understand the purpose and effectiveness of seeing things how they truly are. When we explore, study, reflect upon, and meditate on the nature of reality, we have at our disposal the nuclear warhead to obliterate the destructive processes explained above. And it does not matter in the least if we are speaking about marriage dramas, work dramas, political dramas, or even internal dramas. When the problem is seen as a misperception of reality, then all dramas' support systems are the same; just their content differs.

One More Angle on the Myth of Reality

A primary challenge to our concept of reality is the idea that "what you see is what you get." This is not only a conception, meaning a thought, but it is also a perception that happens in real time. Well, that "real time" is the whole problem. Recently, in the field of neuropsychology, the whole understanding of perception is being turned on its head. Perception and experience within consciousness are being observed and measured quite differently than what has been understood previously. And this new realization in the science community has been a basic understanding within Buddhist psychology for millennia.

Thanks to recent research, it is now understood that what is actually perceived by the senses—and it can vary depending on the sense organ—is not actually incorporated into conscious awareness for five hundred milliseconds. That's about a half of a second. This may not seem long, but what it means is that while we think we are interacting with the present moment, we are in fact interacting, always, with the past. So again, "reality" is not what we are dealing with.

As we touched upon earlier, in Buddhist psychology it is explained that we interact with the world through our five senses: eyes/sight (visual), ears/sound (auditory), nose/smell (odors), tongue/taste (gustatory), and body/touch (sensation). When we perceive something, say our coffee mug, we actually do not experience the mug itself. Rather, the mug appears to our consciousness through the interaction of the mug—its shape, color, and so on—and the eye organ, and then the consciousness, or mind and brain. But what the mind and brain cognize or experience is an image of the mug, not the mug itself. It is like interacting with a photograph of the mug. While we may have a raw, bare, or pure perception of the mug, this is not what we experience in our consciousness and not what we interact with. When we comment to the person handing us our cup of coffee that we actually wanted the bigger mug of coffee, we are not really communicating our actual experience at all, because we are expressing our desire from an image and not the actual object.

While this may sound like splitting hairs, it actually becomes much more profound in everyday life. The reason things become confusing in communication is because often the mental image I generate can be held differently than the mental image you generate. Your mental image, or your relationship with the object, leads you to believe that the mug is plenty big enough, and you don't see why I see it as too small. Our mental images, both actually arising from a moment's past perception, may not be all that different from each other. But our interpretation of the mug, the thing that happens next, almost simultaneously with the erroneous belief that we are seeing things as they are, is a further departure from reality. We interpret the mug, its bigness or smallness, its suitability or unsuitability, based upon a sensation, which is another split-second experience arising in the consciousness. This interpretation of the mug is experienced as true and in the present. But all of these conscious experiences are happening serially and thus are not happening in the same moment, even though our brain and mind believe they are happening all at once, simultaneously. When a meditator deepens their practice, they can actually see this serial unwinding of experience. Everything slows down for them, and they can see that what they thought was real is sorely flawed. Each and every countless perception that happens throughout the day and throughout our life happens in this kind of sequence. The result of such an insight, even if it happens just once, is immensely valuable. And it is why, as Milarepa admonished Gampopa, we must practice!

2
The Myth of Identity

As I mentioned in the previous chapter, Buddhist discourse puts a lot of stock in defining terms before we use them. In this way, the definition of something is an all-important first step on the journey to comprehending it. So how do we define identity? When we speak of identity, we are speaking about the "I," the "self," or "me." It is that thing we refer to when we think of who we are, the person who reacts to situations all day long. Our identity is who we think we are that makes us separate, unique, and distinctive from all other living beings.

Try this: Imagine yourself in a lecture hall, or even just walking down the street, and someone calls out your name. When your name is called out, you have a kind of visceral reaction: "He's pointing out *me*." No one else is around by that name. Your experience is unique in that room. You feel a sense of tightness in your chest perhaps. Or your brain is sort of poked. No one in that room has that strong sense of "I" or "me" like you do. That "I" that is unique to you, that sense of "self," that personal perception of your personality, is what is being referred to here as identity. It is the subject in all you experience.

It's not just what makes you unique, though. It is central to who you think you are. It is the thing that feels sick, feels happy, feels hungry, feels beautiful, feels irritated, feels pleased. In fact, with all of these experiences, and just about every experience, we typically don't say "I feel happy," but "I am happy." So we are not having an experience of being that "I"—we literally are that "I." Even if we say "I feel" or "I think," the subject, the self or "I," believes it is identical with the thing it feels.

The sense of self, one's sense of identity, is constant and imbued in every experience, every breath, every heartbeat—even if it does seem to be quiet much of the time and rather subtle. There is never a time when we are not experiencing the world, and this experiencer is what we're referring to as the identity, the self, the "I." So if you are confused about what this "identity" is, then the easiest thing to do is to turn your gaze inward and examine: *Who is experiencing your world moment to moment?*

Let's look at my day yesterday as an example. Yesterday I went to visit my son and eleven-month-old grandson. I drove the two hours with my wife. I visited with my son and his wife. I played with our grandson. I took him for a walk. My wife and I left in the early evening and drove into San Francisco on our way home. I got agitated from not being able to find a parking spot. I finally found a spot, and I parked the car. I walked with my daughter to the restaurant, and I calmed down from driving around the block. I had dinner with my wife, my daughter, and her boyfriend. I had appetizers that I dug into because I was hungry. I enjoyed my main course. I got anxious to leave as it was getting late and I still had an hour and a half drive home.

As you recount this story with me, do you see how many "I"s there are in such a short time? Open your mind to your present life and think of all the different ways the "I" shows up in just one day. And then reflect on all the days you've lived so far, all the way back to when you were an infant. That is an almost uncountable amount of "I"s or identities or selves that have manifested. And yet, am I literally millions of Karunas (add your name here) or one? The myth of identity then is that we constantly appear to ourselves as just one monolithic, independent, permanent self. But it is impossible that this is the reality. Surely we are not the same "self" as we were in third grade.

Western psychology does not offer us much help here in the form of a clear perspective from which to view reality as it is. Most of the systems we have inherited are concerned with exactly the opposite, in fact: our sense of self, those beliefs that contribute to thinking "I am a certain person." We refer to our self, our identity, our "I" and "mine," unceasingly, but what is this self? Are you who you are because you like a certain set of things? Are you who you are because you feel a certain way today or because you're looking forward to trying that new restaurant? Are you who you are because you're an experienced businessperson—and someone else with less of a track record won't listen to you? Are you who you are because you are madly in love with someone, even as she hardly seems to notice you? Or are you who you are because you've received certain traumas and now your psyche is damaged, and you feel like you can't change? On the fundamental level, that traumatized self appears as independent, solid, and permanent. The intervention is to try to find that traumatized self, but eventually we discover it does not exist. It's merely conceptual.

Three Root Concepts

We constantly say "I" this and "I" that, but do we ever really stop and wonder what the heck this "I" is? The Buddhists do. They do because they believe it is the source of all of our problems—long-term problems as well as short-term problems.

When looking at the myth of identity, there are three concepts that offer an introduction to this profound teaching. They are the belief in the independence of a solid self, the belief in a self that is monolithic and has no parts, and the belief in a self that is permanent. These are the basic or fundamental concepts that are taught as to the nonexistence of an inherently existing self.

Belief in the independence of a solid self

The self, person, or identity is falsely conceived by all of us. We see a self or identity as something concrete, solid, and existing in its own right as some independent authority within our head. We've always thought of it that way, but it is a pure fantasy. It's like a mirage. A mirage exists, the self exists, but not how we think or perceive them to exist. When we are tricked by the mirage of an oasis in the desert, for example, we will walk toward the water we want to drink until we collapse. I think we can all admit that that pursuit would be painful to watch in another person and painful for us to be the victim of. The relief from that "suffering" or "problem" would be to recognize the mirage as a mirage, and thus be able to do what we could to survive and find a proper source of hydration elsewhere.

Just like the example of the mirage, the way we perceive our most cherished self is also a hallucination. And yet, we continually, without break, cater to the whims and desires of this fantasy self. This does not mean there is not a correct self, for surely we do exist! But the *way* we truly exist (in reality) and the way we function to support the way we think we exist are totally, 100 percent non-aligned. This is a habit we've created since beginningless time, so it is a habit that takes constant whittling away at.

In Buddhist psychology the identity is a mere construction, even though it appears, as I said above, as an independent entity, sort of like the king of a country. By *construction*, what is implied is that it is a dependent entity rather than the independent entity it appears to us as. Seeing this takes some dedicated introspection.

If something is constructed, it means it is dependent on the elements and parts of its construction. And if it is dependent, it cannot at the same time be independent. The two, dependency and independence, are mutually exclusive. For example, think about your job. If you are a teacher, then when someone asks you what you do for a living, you'll most likely say, "I'm a teacher." We don't typically say, "I teach," which would be a more accurate reply to "What do you do?" It is important to make this distinction that what we do—as a teacher, student, lawyer, gardener, server, doctor—is inseparable from how we think about ourselves. It becomes our identity. And this identity is felt to be "me." It is perceived as something that really exists on its own, monolithically, without parts, independently. It also appears to be unchanging, permanent, solid, and concrete.

If you tell someone, "I'm a real estate agent," your sense of identity will also be presented. While it is being presented, one can't help but also become emotionally attached to that identity. Now, real estate is something you do, but when the person comments, "Oh, you must not be so good at what you do since I don't see any listings by you." You feel hurt, angry, or defensive. It is as if they are attacking your identity. But if one's identity were independent and stood on its own, it would not be dependent on how many listings were visible or how many homes you sold, because one's identity as an agent would be untouched by any criticism or praise. What this means is that due to my misunderstanding of how my identity exists—as self-existent rather than a mere construction—it is constantly in danger of being hurt or threatened. Because I believe I am my self-identity, I am tricked into reacting and protecting something that is in constant need of support, even though it presents itself as independent. If it is actually a constructed thing, meaning it is dependent upon all kinds of factors—like how many listings it has, its education level, the size of its office, the kind of car it drives, its annual income from sales, how many phone inquiries it gets each week, how many houses it shows each month—then this independent identity is not independent at all. It's a ruse. A hallucination that I cater to by serving and building it up every moment of the day.

If this self were an independent entity, then how do I explain that I have multiple selves? It seems I've got multiple personalities. I am a student. I am a psychotherapist. I am a teacher. I am a father. I am a husband. I am an American. I was a son, but now that my parents have died, am I no longer a son? I am a writer. When I was young, I was a backpacker, a surfer, a hippie. At those times, those identities seemed independent, permanent, solid. Did those guys pass away? If so, how is it I'm still here? When reflecting on one's identity, when it arises it feels permanent, fixed, unchanging. If that were so, however, then how can it change from father one minute to writer the next?

Let's look at another example. I am a father of three adult children. Before I had kids, I did not have the label "father." Further than that, of course, I did not have the identity "father." This identity of father, when in my father identity, seems fixed, unchanging. If that were so, how did it happen that one minute before my first son was born I was not a father, and then a minute later I became one? Something that is permanent means it is unchanging. How did this unchanging thing suddenly change? It makes no sense.

Where this becomes especially significant is when our emotions and mental well-being are affected by how we think about our identity, by what people say about this identity, by how we perceive our identity and how others perceive us—that is, the whole question of self-worth. It looks like this: When my kids were young, I was their hero, a great father. When they matured and we had conflicts, my standing as their hero slowly, or not so slowly, dissolved. Then as they became adults and our relationship dynamic changed again, I was "hero-dad" again. In other words, how they saw my father identity and how I perceived myself as a father was, and is, completely conditional. Again, if the identity is an independent entity, then it cannot be dependent on conditions. So here we have a problem with the identity not only appearing as permanent but independent as well. For something to be independent, it cannot be dependent on conditions. This paradox is in play with any and all of our so-called self-images or identities.

The myth of identity then should cause us to reconsider any conclusions that originate with the phrase "I am a . . ." I am a Democrat. I am a Republican. I am a Christian. I am an atheist. To hold on to an identity so-named is to obscure how we came to that identity, not to mention all of the things we don't share in common with that identity. Yet we cling to that identity nonetheless, and then ascribe further labels on top of it. It is not enough to be a businessperson, an artist, a parent, or an athlete. We further grasp at our identity by saying we are "a successful businessperson," "a talented artist," "a failure as a parent," "a frustrated athlete," and so on. Thinking of ourselves as something fixed, unchanging, and independent of everything else—the three key elements of the myth of identity—leads to unhappiness as we both adhere to one particular identity and then ascribe to it unrealistic qualities, both negative and positive.

This fixed, unchanging, independent self is completely false, but we believe in it anyway. We are compelled through habit to think this way. Then when someone threatens our sense of identity—"Democrats are a bunch of spendthrifts," or "If you were a better mother, your child would be less disruptive in class"—we have a negative reaction. Our mind becomes disturbed. Depression, anxiety, loss, fear, anger, and so on need a solid identity to adhere to. But identity itself is constantly changing; identity arises, abides, and diminishes every instant. Trying to stick a label onto an apparently independent self—that is, in fact, fluid—is like putting a Post-it on flowing water. It's impossible. Without the concept of a solid, concrete identity, then the "Post-its"—emotions, thoughts, feelings, and beliefs—cannot stick.

When we begin to unravel the misconception of identity, what might also be called "the tricks of the ego," it may seem that full mental health or awakening will be the result of the annihilation of the ego altogether. We might think that we will just sort of disappear into the void, that we cease to exist at all. But these ideas, too, are an exaggeration, and we need to be especially mindful of them in our quest to tame the ego and see through the myth of identity.

Lama Yeshe used to say, "You need a healthy ego to practice the Buddhist path." I thought the goal was to eliminate the ego, subdue it, and see it for what it is—a mere hallucination, a constructed entity, and not some monolithic source of salvation. So what did Lama Yeshe mean?

It must have been in the late seventies or early eighties when there was an event at Kopan Monastery in Nepal that shed some light on the paradoxical message of needing a healthy ego to subdue the ego. The monastery's annual November Course would attract around two hundred curious travelers, backpackers, Dharma bums, and hippies from all over the world. We were one of the few places in Asia in those days where a foreigner could study Buddhism in English. It was the early pioneer days and conditions were tough, especially with

Nepal being one of the poorest countries in the world at the time. There was no running water, infrequent and basic electricity, no phones, straw mats for bedding, and lots and lots of fleas. But I must say it was this tough environment that made Nepal so special, so charming, so exotic. It is hard to describe, but I had the same sense of contentment that one experiences hiking in the wilderness with few belongings. It called for a simpler mindset.

I remember vividly at one November Course there was a German woman who was having what I learned later in my clinical psychology studies was a brief psychotic disorder. This can and does happen when people engage in meditation practices that are either too advanced for their nervous system or are done incorrectly. When she applied to attend the course, there were no indications she had any mental health challenges. Several days into the course, however, she started to manifest bizarre behavior. I remember her sitting on a wall, and as people passed by, she hissed at them and made gestures with her tongue as if she were a snake. It was quite intimidating. Her behavior escalated to where she started to break some windows in the temple and other shrines on the property.

As I was the primary manager for the course, I went to consult with Lama Yeshe as to what action we should take. It was not so clear-cut what the proper response should be as it might be in the US today. There were no mental health hotlines then—there were barely any telephones—and no internet to research how to help, nor any emergency mental health clinics or services.

In some people's minds, a Tibetan Buddhist monastery might be considered the ideal haven for a person going through this kind of experience. When I went to consult with Lama Yeshe, I stood outside his door listening to a conversation he was having with the course leader, an American nun. The course leader was saying something to the effect that being in the monastery was the right place for this woman to process her struggle. But Lama was saying she had to leave. Lama emphasized she needed help that the monastery could not provide. The American nun pushed back. If you knew Lama Yeshe, you'd know pushing back was probably a mistake. You could have a discussion with him, a dialogue—but an argument? He was way too good at that, having trained for decades in the art of debate. Their conversation went like this:

> Nun: But Lama, we're a monastery. A refuge. How can we send her out?
>
> Lama: She needs help, dear.
>
> Nun: Here we are taught daily about compassion to all living beings. This must be the right place for her to be for help.
>
> Lama (forcefully): She needs to go to the hospital!
>
> Nun: Lama, the hospitals here are basic and primitive.
>
> Lama (more forcefully): She needs a doctor! Take her to the hospital.
>
> Nun: But Lama . . .
>
> Lama (with a strong voice and slamming his hand on a table for emphasis): She needs a psychiatrist! Take her to the hospital now! ***Buddhism is for healthy people, dear!***

There are many lessons here. One, maybe not the most important, is that Buddhism is not for everyone. That is why the Dalai Lama often says how wonderful it is that there are so many different religions and paths, so that there is more opportunity for everyone to find a spiritual path, or a healing path, that is suitable for their temperament.

The second lesson, and the one perhaps more germane to this discussion, is that one needs a "healthy" ego to subdue the ego. Like the woman above, if you are out of touch with conventional reality, you are just superimposing one hallucination on top of another. According to Buddhist philosophy and psychology, our main obstacle to full awakening and health is ignorance. This ignorance is already projecting a reality that is "untrue," yet which we ascribe to and believe is true. So superimposing another, more extreme, perhaps, reality on top of that is double ignorance—and double suffering.

Belief in a self that is monolithic and has no parts

Following from the above discussion then, there is no absolute "I" or "me," but there is a relative one. Of course, there is someone who practices the path and becomes awakened. But that "someone" is not the usual one we refer to. The someone who becomes awakened is a relative being, conditional and relational—not someone who is fixed, unchanging, and independent.

Identity is not something that exists on its own. Yet when we do some simple self-analysis, we will see that our belief is that our identity does appear to exist independently, on its own, as a sort of monolith. This is a very deep, profound topic and essential to contemplate if we're to progress along the journey to complete freedom. This is a deeper phase of the journey than therapy can take us. Modern psychological theory has not yet articulated a clear, deep, thorough understanding of identity. It is a new science and thus has a bit to go before it can offer us a full approach to inner fulfillment. Modern therapy does work well for temporal, immediate problems, such as relationship struggles, communication difficulties, mental health crises, suicide prevention, and the early stages of treating alcohol and substance abuse. However, when we get to the deeper purpose of psychology—the complete and permanent elimination of mental and emotional distress—modern psychology falls tremendously short.

Again, I'm not speaking about shorter-term improvement. It was interesting to me when, in the nineties, California allocated funding for a "self-esteem" initiative. This initiative was to offer public funding for schools and other programs to help children raise their self-esteem. This was a well-intentioned effort, I suppose, to help children become more confident and self-assured. These are not bad aims when put in the proper context. Many people have a history of being victims of verbal, physical, emotional, and sexual abuse, the effects of which are the development of a self-image of weakness and unworthiness. One can often feel unlovable and flawed. In these cases, often we would say that the person does not have a "healthy ego," and modern therapeutic practices are well-suited for this kind of condition. The ego needs some building up to become healthy and more functional. A person needs to reconstruct their self-image from one of disdain, weakness, and defectiveness to one in which the person has self-respect, self-affection, and courage.

Beyond this, though, Western psychology can actually make things worse in the long run, according to the Buddhist psychologist, when it strengthens a person's attachment to an identity that is reputed to be indivisible. This is because the idea that one is an independent entity can be extended to include others besides yourself. In other words, to the extent we reify our own independence, we then project the same degree of an independent identity onto others. This may be fine when we are aware of this dynamic and have a degree of doubt that the way we are identifying them, and ourselves, is a misperception. But when we believe in ourselves and others as strongly existent, independent entities, then it is to that degree we will defend that belief, fight for it, and hang on to it—and do the same for the way we describe that identity or personality.

The efforts behind slogans such as "Make America Great Again" are dominated by the myth of identity—but they do little to recognize that "American culture" is a construction of parts from countless different cultures. Nationalist independence lies in direct contradiction to the fact of global interdependence, which we can see on every level, from the transmission of a virus to the effect of increased greenhouse gas emissions to the interlocking concerns of international monetary funds. These cultural or conventional examples are one way of understanding how belief in the myth of identity informs every aspect of our lives.

When we believe in the myth of identity, we open

ourselves to all kinds of global catastrophes like climate destruction and nationalist fervor; we might even end up killing someone—whether that killing is governmentally sanctioned or not. We can only kill someone when we are very far into the dark edges of the myth of identity. If, on the other hand, we see everyone as interconnected and everything as interdependent, it's just not possible to harm others.

We apply the myth of identity to everything, including and especially people: our girlfriend, our children, our boss, the guy who's going slow in the fast lane—and, most of all, ourselves. By seeing others as completely independent of ourselves, it becomes much easier to objectify them and thus justify harming them, stealing from them, repressing them, and so forth.

Even a thought such as "My side is more important than your side" indicates there are multiple sides that make up a whole. Every attempt at independence implies by its nature a dependence. Dependence is a truth, like gravity. It is present on the global level, the cultural level, the familial level, and the level of the personality, where the myth of identity leads us into behaviors designed to protect the well-being of our seemingly discrete "self," "soul," or "ego." This, in turn, feeds the growing attitude of entitlement—we believe we have a right to a good job, a loving partner, and constitutional freedoms such as life, liberty, and the pursuit of happiness—whether or not we give any regard to our dependence on others for that happiness or well-being.

Counter to the myth of identity is the truth of interdependence. There is nothing that exists independently, all on its own; everything is conditional or relational.

Relational means "in relationship." This implies a dependency. There is no relationship without two things, or more, that make up the relationship. Therefore, *relational* or a *relationship* is dependent, implying that at least two things that exist because of or in dependence on each other. If they are dependent, they are naturally not independent: they are unable to exist on their own. For example, I am a husband because that label is dependent on having a wife. No wife, no husband. A table looks like an independent entity, but that's because we don't really perceive or attend to the fact that it is a dependent thing. In a way, we would say the table is "relational" as it is in relationship to its legs, its surface, the floor it rests on, its color, and many other factors. To perceive a table in this way, without all the mental gymnastics and thinking, would be a more accurate way of seeing it—rather than as an independent entity, which is our normal perception.

The entire world, outer and inner, is relational, dependent, and yet we do not see anything that way—the way that things actually exist. We can apply this to the parts of our own body as we move past the view we hold of it being some sort of separate entity. We can then contemplate all the ways our thoughts and emotions are interdependent. Finally, we can look at the world around us and contemplate the interdependence that exists between us and both animate and inanimate objects.

Before we leave the subject of the self being monolithic, allow me to recount another experience I had at Kopan Monastery. The practice of contemplation has been perfected by the Tibetans, and the earlier Indian scholars and contemplatives, in their training through debate. Debate in the monasteries looks very little like the debate we are familiar with in colleges and debate clubs, and nothing at all like what is called "debate" in the political realm. In order to sharpen their intellect and contemplative skills, monks will first, as young adepts, memorize many different debate scenarios and topics. These debates are highly formulaic and only become creative once the monks mature both in age and education. The debate session is highly formalized and yet dynamic. The training involves debate partners having to take both sides of an argument and defend each one. The topics are philosophical and often go to the very depths of questioning the nature of reality as it is expressed by different philosophical schools. The monks thus develop a highly refined quality of being able to dissect and look at any philosophical or moral topic.

I could always tell when the young monks were beginning to connect with their study of debate. At times, just to drive me nuts, they'd begin debates if I were even to ask where, say, Tenzin was.

"Who is Tenzin?" they'd bait me.

"You know who Tenzin is. The one who works in the office," I'd volunteer as a willing victim.

"What does he look like?" they'd prompt.

"He's tall and thin, and the brother of Lobsang."

"I see; so you are saying Tenzin is the body called 'Tenzin'?"

Well, now I was trapped. "Yes," I'd say.

"So you're saying Tenzin is his body. That's Tenzin? So when Tenzin dies, you'll still call him Tenzin till his body decays? Is he Tenzin if you preserve his body?"

"No, Tenzin is his mind?" I'd offer, knowing full well the response that would bring.

"Oh! So you're looking for Tenzin the mind and not the body?"

I could say both, to which they'd reply, "So there are two Tenzins? One who is the body and one who is the mind?"

"No, they are dependent on one and the other."

"So," they would ask, "How many parts do you want to attribute to this entity called 'Tenzin'? Is there one Tenzin or many?"

The rest of the conversation would take a full chapter to explain and, by that time, I'd go off on my own to look for Tenzin.

Belief in a self that is permanent

In the next chapter, we will take up the myth of permanence, but I believe a precursor may be useful here, as it is also relevant to misperceptions about the self. The third aspect of the myth of identity is belief in a self that is permanent. If the self were permanent, then it would not change. (*Permanent* here does not mean eternal, but unchanging.) There is very little that is permanent in the universe, and yet we exactly relate to our sense of self as a permanent, unchanging entity. This is a hallucination that we believe and adhere to every moment of our life.

But this does not mean that our goal in exploring the myth of identity is to completely annihilate ourselves. What would be the fun in that? There'd be no purpose if the idea were to completely vaporize and become nonexistent. The Buddha himself would not exist and, surely, could be seen as some sort of executioner of human existence—and for what reason?

So let me be clear: *We are engaged in a process of uncovering, and discovering, the unhealthy ego that keeps us from experiencing complete fulfillment as human beings.* That unhealthy ego, or self-identity, is not our complete being. In fact, that misconception of oneself is the thing that prevents us from reaching our full human potential. That human potential, when we actualize it in whole or in part, or even while we are in the process of realizing it, is a state of wellness, joy, and wisdom that exceeds our wildest dreams. But we have to work for it. And while it may be a "God-given right," it is not handed to us on a silver platter by God or by the Buddha. It is our job to uncover it.

There is a "true" self and a "false" self. We have discussed the false self up to now. The "true" self is put in quotes for a reason, because the word *true* is used in a conditional sense and not an absolute sense. There is no absolute "I" or "me," but there is a relative one. This relative self is the you that has traveled through endless lifetimes to get where you are now and will continue to travel forever—either as a confused being, as it has until now, or as an awakening and eventually an awakened being. Rather than being afraid that this relative self is a mere construction, we can experience the benefits of such a situation. As Lama Yeshe used to say, since it is a construction, you have the freedom to construct it into something much more fulfilling than the usual self-pitying, unfulfilling life we might typically find in our reflections. If we see something as illusory, it gives us the prospect of just creating a better illusion.

Fully understanding the myth of identity allows us to be completely fluid with the way we approach our life, our problems, our joys, and loves. When we no longer have to be stuck on one identity because we understand the lack of solidity in all of our identities, we take control of how and who we wish to be. It is truly liberating. It is an awakening into our true nature, and not only that, a new sense of empowerment takes over. Rather than emotions, events, thoughts, and people telling us who we are, we get to choose—and we can choose an identity that is more awakened and more alive.

3
The Myth of Permanence

The Buddha was walking through a village in India when a distraught woman approached him. As she held her dead infant in her arms, she begged him to bring the child back to life. She had heard of his miraculous abilities and believed he could relieve her of this most dreadful situation.

The Buddha calmly promised her that he would bring her baby back to life if she would bring him a handful of mustard seeds from a home in the village that had never experienced a death in the family. Some time later she returned, empty-handed, but understanding deeply that all families are touched by grief like her own. In fact, even the Buddha cannot bestow immortality or release someone from the law of impermanence. Unlike other traditions that believe in an omnipotent god, Buddhism discounts this belief. The Buddha is awakened but not omnipotent; the same can be said for the state of mind called "buddhahood" or "enlightenment."

Not long ago I was in Nepal working with my teacher Lama Zopa Rinpoche. As he stood up to leave our meeting, he said, "You see, people get up and see everything as permanent. As they walk toward the bathroom they still see permanence. When they're in the bathroom, they still see permanence. As they leave the bathroom and go through the doorway, they still see permanence. Then they might die then and there, and right up to that point they still see permanence."

His point, of course, was that there is nothing static in that whole event. Not even for a nanosecond. And even hearing that from him, I was still not prepared when, a few months later, on April 13, 2023, Lama Zopa would pass away. After hearing of his passing, one of the first memories that echoed in my mind was him giving the above exposition. I could see him telling us this as if it were happening again, anew. I couldn't help thinking that he gave that explanation during one of the last conversations I had with him after a forty-eight-year relationship purposely about his own impending departure.

Because of his level of meditative experience, Lama Zopa never slept, never got "burned out," and never felt depressed. In a public talk he was once asked, "What do you do to relax?" He responded, "I practice morality." He always expressed joy, even when he had experienced a stroke some ten years earlier. When his breathing stopped and after attempts to resuscitate him were unsuccessful, he was situated in a sitting position on his meditation cushion. There he sat in a deep meditative state, looking exactly as he had been seen countless times. For three days he sat there without any smell or signs of decomposition. His attendants even reported a sweet aroma coming from his body. After three days, a drop of blood appeared from his left nostril. In the Buddhist scientific literature on the death process, this is a sign that the subtle consciousness has now left the body and the person has entered the intermediate state prior to the next rebirth.

Lama Zopa said many times that for very advanced meditators, death is like a holiday. This is, in part, due to the advances that can be made in one's spiritual development as a result of being able to enter a meditative state that is extremely subtle in death, since all the coarse emotions and thoughts have subsided. This is a state of ultimate peace. But make no mistake; unless one has trained in this practice for a very long time, there is no way to take advantage of this refined state of consciousness where breathing and blood flow have stopped. Advanced meditators are able to stop their breathing for hours while still maintaining meditative equipoise and super-awareness.

Is There Anything Permanent?

Just as the death of Lama Zopa brought the myth of permanence home to me again, so have we all experienced losses that remind us anew that nothing lasts forever. This is a very rudimentary understanding of the law of impermanence. When we believe in the myth of permanence, we ignore both scientific and psychological facts to grasp on to situations, people, ways of being, and conceptions that feel familiar even if they are dysfunctional or destructive. We insist on this permanence because it provides comfort, despite all the evidence to the contrary. As Geshe Gelek said, "We see what isn't there and we don't see what is there." What we see—what we perceive with all our five senses and our mind that is not there—is permanence.

As always, we will want to define our terms before proceeding too far into a discussion of the myth of permanence. In common use, *permanence* is often used interchangeably with the word *eternal*. In Buddhist philosophy, however, *permanence* is defined as "a nonproduct," something not produced. In essence, and perhaps more easily understood, a permanent thing is something that does not change from moment to moment. Impermanence rather is that which is produced; it is a product. That means it is subject to cause and effect and is constantly in a state of change, whether we see that change or not.

There are very few phenomena that are permanent, but they exist. We are not so concerned here with the permanent, but an example of a permanent phenomenon is space. Space does not change moment to moment. It is nonatomic. It is the space between the atoms one could say. When we look at the sky, we might see blue. That is not space. That is the reflection of the water crystals in the space of sky—something having to do with atoms. If there were no space, we could not have water crystals, could we? But this part of the discussion is not where we want to focus, at least not at the moment. Impermanence, on the other hand, includes atomic things, but also nonatomic things like thoughts, feelings, emotions, and other "mental stuff."

Nonatomic Impermanence

What distinguishes the impermanent from the permanent is that the impermanent changes from moment to moment and is subject to cause and effect. Our state of mind is up and down, not stable, for example. While a specific number of perceptions per second is elusive, research suggests our brains are incredibly active, constantly receiving and filtering sensory data. Some studies hint at perception cycles operating on timescales of milliseconds, meaning we could be having hundreds or even thousands of microperceptions every second. However, most of these likely remain below conscious awareness. Every microsecond of perception means the mind is moving even at the microsecond level. This creates suffering, because when our state of mind changes so frequently, every instant, we have no solid foundation or personal philosophy to depend on for any length of time. We yearn for any appearance of solidity and reliability, not appreciating that the mind can be moved from the heavens to the hells in a split second. While we want real, solid ground beneath our feet, so to say, it needs to be reliable, yes, but also flexible and fluid. It is more helpful to go through life like we're surfing rather than trying to cement our feet in the ground, trying to be stable in a continually shifting environment with an ever-changing mind.

I remember one of my biggest light bulb moments came when I was just one mile from the epicenter of the 1989 earthquake in the San Francisco Bay Area. I could not make sense of the very thing I thought was stablest and most reliable, one of the things that seemed permanent: the ground beneath my feet was now shaking and rolling. The street looked like a ribbon in the wind as opposed to the solid, unmoving structure I always thought it was. If you cannot trust the earth under your feet, then what can you trust?

Most of us are aware, on some level, that things are in a constant state of flux. We know this, but there is a difference between what we know to be true and how we live. We know that spring flows into summer and summer into autumn. We know that we will eventually retire from our careers. We know our kids are going to leave home when they grow up, and that we'll have to someday replace that worn-out appliance. We know that our shiny new car, with its comfortable upholstery, will become dated and lose its allure. But we live as if these things will last forever, as if this new friendship we are so excited about isn't going to lose its luster or our parents aren't going to die or our job is static and secure.

We mistakenly, and habitually, believe that what we are experiencing is not subject to the nature of change. We then cling to this good, or bad, feeling as if it were fixed, solid, and unchanging. Disappointment and distress follow once the feeling does change (or relief, if a bad feeling has been alleviated). And throughout it all, we are constantly taken by surprise even though the very nature of feeling is flux. We give lip service to the fact that everything changes, but we do not live respecting this law. It is just intellectual. It is not an object of perception or experience. We literally do not see it; it is not an object of our perception. The law of impermanence for us is not experiential. And because we respond to what we see or perceive, we are always misled.

You may be thinking even now that this is all very interesting, but really it is useless, other than as an intellectual pursuit, as it does not have real-life implications. Well, the implications are huge. Remember that our goal here is to live happier, more fulfilled lives. The Buddhist premise is that this is achievable only by gracing the mind with wisdom. In other words, wisdom is the key to happiness. The wisdom we speak about in Buddhism is the wisdom of what and how things exist. Let's put this to the test.

The other day my mind got quite disturbed when advice I had given on a project I was consulting for was not only disregarded, but contradictory advice was followed. I could foresee the negative fallout from not following the advice I was providing. Worse yet, the exact opposite advice was being promulgated instead. I just could see a disaster unfolding before me as, from what I perceived, the person in charge was maneuvering with a sense of arrogance and political motivation rather than thoughtfulness and concern for all.

I was upset and angry. But if I had had a direct perception of impermanence, as opposed to just an intellectual or conceptual one, I would not have gotten hooked by the situation. The mind is constantly grasping at what it perceives—sounds, smells, tastes, sensations, shapes, and colors, as well as all thoughts, dreams, ideas, images, and so forth. Not only does it see these objects as static when they are not, it then tries to *hold* them as static. Dissatisfaction will inevitably arise as we lose the thing we are hoping will give us some positive experience. It was only because I saw what wasn't there instead of seeing what was there that I became subsumed, again, into the unending problem cycle. The whole context, the entire situation before me, was impermanent, moving, fluid, nonstatic, nonconcrete. Yet all I saw was everything appearing as fixed, unmoving, inert, solid. And from that, anger had ground to take root. It was almost like anger suddenly had the conditions, perhaps permission, to come into play.

It is not change that is the problem at all. Change is the constant nature of the mind. It is the mind's habitual grasping to hold and preserve elements, experiences, sensations, images, and other things that are in a constant state of change that is the problem. This is the meaning of *grasping*. In fact, it is not so much the desire for things that is the problem, but the grasping to keep something. In this way, the myth of permanence fuels our attachment, whereas an embrace of the law of constant change is the route to freedom—in any given moment and throughout one's lifetime.

Two Levels of Impermanence

There are two levels of impermanence: *gross*, or as we might refer to it, *coarse*, and *subtle*. The above examples demonstrate coarse impermanence: death, changing seasons, retirement. Subtle impermanence is more profound and even more essential to understand. There is no coarse impermanence without subtle impermanence. Subtle impermanence is the actual law of change. Atoms and molecules are constantly in movement—arising, abiding, and decaying—and are the foundation for larger things to disintegrate and cease to exist. In the exact same way, our mind, emotions, thoughts, and feelings are also in constant movement and change. Everything, including the subject, this "I," is moving more quickly than the instant. The deep meditator can perceive impermanence through watching the mind move moment to moment. Even if you and I cannot initially conceive impermanence, we can talk about it in a logical way. And then, eventually, when you are going for a walk or talking to your sister, you can notice that things are changing moment to moment. Meditation comes down to direct experience. When the mind quiets enough, you can have an insight into impermanence—you can directly perceive it, like gravity: *Oh, there it is!* In this way, the law of impermanence is similar to the law of cause and effect, the focus of our next myth.

Coarse impermanence, however, is where most of us start. We are all familiar with coarse impermanence even though we don't really respect it. Coarse impermanence is the sense of things changing over time. We come out of our house one day and notice that it needs a new coat of paint. Or our car is finally breaking down and needs to be replaced. If we take a slightly broader view, our children, who seemed to just be toddlers a few days ago, are now headed off to college. The ocean, we've noticed, has worn away the cliffs. The seasons have changed, and now it seems to be cold and rainy. That makes us sad, but if we think about it, we know spring and summer will come a few months after that. Our parents seem to be less vibrant and sharp, and we wonder when that started. The promotion we finally got is now moving us closer to retirement. The neighborhood seems to be changing—houses are become more expensive or more rundown; they are building in all the free space, which seems to be making things much more congested; when did the traffic become so bad? Coarse impermanence can be seen by the senses, even if we pay just a little attention to it. And the recognition of coarse impermanence is immensely important.

It is interesting that even this obvious law, a law that anyone can perceive, is still almost completely ignored. For example, when we buy a new car we are so enamored by it, so hypnotized by permanence, that we see the car as something completely enticing. It will last that way *forever.* When we look at the new car, we see only the new and attractive image. And we see it that way as a truth. It really is new and shiny and attractive. But if that were true, then the car would forever stay in that condition; if the car itself were permanently enticing and fun, then we'd always see it that way. We know this won't be the case, however. Even if the car is preserved quite well, when it shows up on the used car lot ten years later, or even sooner, almost no one is enamored or relates to it in the same way as when it was new. Why? It is very important to realize here that I am talking not about an intellectual analysis but the default of how the mind creates, perceives, and believes its reality.

I noticed when Teslas first hit the market, so many people were intrigued. It seemed to me people were impressed and excited by their technology, design, and performance. Then I recalled how not that many years before, we felt the exact same way when the Prius was introduced. We made many of the same comments, being impressed about the design or the new technology. And now? My point is that the same awe you got when you (and me, of course) looked at the Prius some years ago, and when we look at the Tesla now, will be the same awe we get when we look at a flying car in the future. Our perspective will still be situated from the view of permanence. We do not look at how these cars are going to be passé in a few years, how someday they are going to appear fairly ordinary even, when in fact they are the exact same objects.

When we think of our next vacation—perhaps a cruise to a foreign country or an exotic trek—we have an image that arises in our mind of the trip. When we research the destination, book the flights, rent the car, or look at the map of the cycling route we plan to take, we see all of that as permanent. Everything that appears to our senses and mind is static. We never look beyond the trip to the post-vacation hangover that comes when we get back to our normal lives and the bills that have to be paid; nor are we thinking of the last time we will show the photographs to someone who may be interested in our travels, or the last time we ourselves will even think about that particular trip. To consider such things in this life feels unbearably sad and depressing. And here, let me say that it is not that one should not enjoy beautiful things and experiences in the world. That is not my point. As Lama Yeshe used to say, "We should enjoy. It's part of being human. Animals can't enjoy like we can. But the problem is we cling. Can we just not cling?" But we always cling. We always try to preserve things as if freezing them will mean our pleasure will endure with it. This belief and pattern of behavior are what is meant by *ignorance*. We are once again seeing something that is just not there the way it is appearing to us—and relying on it even. What *is* there is the law of impermanence—not only do objects change, but because the mind and the object are interdependent, our mind changes with the object.

This pattern of clinging to what appears before us, both "out there" and internally in our mind, is something we engage with every moment of our lives. We may think, *So what?* The "so what" is remembering that, fundamentally, every living thing wants to be happy, and hopscotching from one pleasure to another is neurotic, unstable, and naturally unfulfilling. Again, I am not speaking out against feeling pleasure or feeling good. That is not the problem; to not feel good would be a waste of this precious human life. Martyrdom is no different than blindly following the pleasant. But if we realize the problem lies with our clinging, like Lama Yeshe said, and our constant misguided search for the things we think make us happy, then everything becomes much clearer. Everything becomes much more peaceful, realistic, and sane.

The moment we cling to our experience—even if it's the experience of the end of the workday and dinner out on the town, sitting back after work with a glass of wine to relax, putting our feet up and watching TV—we are going to be let down, as these experiences fade away. The next workday comes, and again we're left wanting to decompress at the end the day. And the cycle just continues. However, if there is no clinging, no attempt to make a moment of pleasure last or endure, then we can just enjoy the moment for what it is and let it fade into the ether of both the material world and the empty spaciousness of our mind. These expereinces become just clouds floating across our reality. So remember: clinging is the problem, and clinging is based upon an incorrect—that is, ignorant—view of reality, of what is presenting itself in our experience . . . every instant.

This brings us to subtle impermanence. The realization of subtle impermanence is life-changing. If there were no subtle impermanence, there would be no coarse impermanence. This is just scientific. For coarse impermanence to take place—the change in seasons, the deterioration of our home, the eventual breaking down of our car, the end of our holiday—there has to be subtle impermanence or change. In the material world, such as the aging of our home and car, this subtle change is occurring constantly. We just can't physically perceive subtle change. But if you put a time-lapse camera on anything material, you can get a sense of the moment-to-moment change. Cars are not permanent fixtures that just one day become junkers. They are always disintegrating; we just don't see it. The atoms and molecules that make up the larger parts are always in a state of flux. This is also true in the context of the inner world of the mind. The advanced meditator can *actually see* subtle impermanence because their mind has slowed down to the extent that they can perceive subtle change.

The mind is very strange. When we think about or plan or get excited about an upcoming holiday or Friday night dinner with friends, it feels like we're engaging with the real thing. When we get angry and disappointed with our kids for bringing home bad grades or trouble they got into at school, we think we're engaging with our real children. Even when we order an omelet at a restaurant and the waiter delivers eggs over easy, the eggs, the waiter, and the restaurant all appear solid and real in our frustration. These people and things all appear to us as permanent, unchanging, static, and fixed. They are not. Psychologically, what is happening is that we are not dealing with any of these objects at all.

Rather, when we engage with the world, what we are actually engaging with is the mind—more specifically, the inner world, the projected images of the mind. While outer objects have some sort of existence, of course, actual experience itself is completely mental. Friday night's dinner, the report card, the eggs, ad infinitum, are mental experiences. While the senses perceive all the objects "out there," everything is interpreted and experienced "in here," in the mind itself. So, bizarrely, when we perceive something—even mental stuff like plans, memories, daydreams, fears, and sadness—everything is seen by the mind as an image of the thing we are perceiving. In other words, we don't engage with the actual object, whether external or internal, but we engage with a mental image of it, a kind of reflection. And that reflection appears as permanent. So, in fact, all the things we love and hate, get irritated by and enjoy, long for and avoid, expect and dread are all nothing but imposters we think of as the real thing. If we were to see the "real" thing, we would be totally relaxed and at ease because we'd see its impermanent nature. This perception does not deny that these reflections have qualities that may be helpful or harmful. I'm not saying nothing matters. Of course, in this relative world we live in, things matter because they produce effects: negative and positive, helpful and harmful. But if we could see them for what they actually are, instead of such solid, self-existent static entities, we'd experience things as fluid—wispy like smoke or liquid like a gently flowing stream. If you try to grasp mist passing before your eyes, you cannot pin it down anywhere. The moment you try to hold it, it is gone, having changed into its next appearance.

On the subtle level of impermanence, when we speak of ignorance, we are speaking about that function of the mind that does not see things as "essenceless"—that is, as in having no essence—because if something is in a constant state of flux, where do you find "the thing"? Instead, we see things as solid and automatically grasp them and hold them as unchanging. If we think of a beautiful flowing river, we can easily imagine how fruitless it would be to try to grasp the water in our hand. Yet it is easier to conceive the water as unholdable than it is to conceive our own mind in the same way. That is simply because we are more educated about the nature of flowing water than the nature of a flowing mind.

The meditator, the spiritual practitioner, is able to so substantially slow their mind down that they can perceive this directly. Instead of things appearing as concrete monoliths, they appear like the soft movements of a dance. This experience is blissful, happy. It is a happiness based upon reality, or a closer version of reality than the fantastic and hallucinated world we relate to and believe is real. This is a flavor of what is meant by *happiness* in Buddhist thought. And Buddhists sages of past and present want us all to wake up and smell the coffee. For them, everything appears like a fantasy, a dream, a magic show. They watch us clamor after, get upset by, and long for a make-believe world that we believe exists solidly, the way it appears. For these wise ones, their natural uncontrived reaction to the dreamlike world is a sense of care and compassion for those of us who continually misinterpret the world and then act upon that misinterpretation. It must be like trying to shout to the moth that it is going to be burned up by the flame it so longingly pursues.

4
The Myth of Randomness

So far, we have learned about a myth that has its exact and opposing law: the myth of permanence and the law of impermanence. In the case of this chapter, the myth of randomness finds its antithesis in the law of causality, what is called *karma* in Sanskrit. The law of causality is a provocation to the Western mindset because generally we have neither knowledge of nor acceptance of cause and effect. We'll discuss why it is such a big lift for us to confront this law below, but suffice it to say that this is so challenging is no more surprising than it was when people first started to accept the law of gravity.

What does *karma* mean? I speak Nepalese, which is a Sanskrit-based language; in Nepal, when we say we are going to do something, we use the word *kar*. Sometimes *karma* is translated as "work." But it's not really work; it's more this kind of action. Karma is activity. As a natural result of this activity, everything is both a cause of something else to come and an effect of something that has happened to the past. It feels very logical when we say it like this, even uplifting. About karma, Lama Yeshe once said, "The more convinced one becomes of the inner law of cause and effect, the more energy one gets to change and improve oneself and one's life."

In my psychotherapy work, however, I have seen many clients struggle with the implications of this concept, which can be staggering. If I am sitting with a couple, perhaps, going through intense problems, even if I and both partners do all of the work we are supposed to do, sometimes nothing changes that much. It occurs to me in such situations, "This karma is too heavy"—meaning the causes are too deep or too extensive within their minds for them to change their habits. What do you do when the causes are deep and well-established? This is a big problem for us modern people, particularly in the mental health professions. We tend to always try to deal with effects rather than the causes for those effects, but this may not be so effective. The spiritual path to creating happiness involves eliminating the causes of unhappiness, not just dealing with the symptoms. Medication cannot cure depression, for example, even though it may provide a very fortunate assist while one works on the causes of the depression. And we do this by confronting one of the myths we live by: the myth of randomness.

The Answer Is Karma

We hold in our awareness the idea that things are random. Sometimes things happen, like a job loss, without warning. When I returned to the United States after being in Nepal for twelve years, I immediately got hired at two colleges to teach English as a second language. I had taught English for years in Nepal and, in fact, had a master's degree in teaching English as a second language.

I was very qualified and hirable. But one of the colleges let me go after a year despite good reviews from the students. I was crestfallen; I had never been fired before, and I could not make sense of the causes. For about two weeks I wallowed in self-doubt and low self-worth until a colleague from the college called me and said, "Karuna, don't take it so hard. They were always going to hire you just for the year until the teacher who was on sabbatical returned. They knew you wouldn't take the job if you knew it was just for one year." It seemed so random, but the conditions of my firing became clear to me. The question of "why that happened to *me*," however, is where karma comes into play. The rest of the reasons are what are referred to as conditions, not the why—that's karma.

Sometimes we express apparent randomness through resorting to a divine intelligence. We say, "God did it. It's God's will." Or to use language that might be more common for some of us, "The universe did it. It's in the universal plan." Many people these days have become nontheistic, so they ascribe omniscience and omnipotence to whatever totality of the cosmos "the universe" is supposed to represent, and post on social media that "the universe has a plan for you," or "the universe will let me know what I need to do."

If we don't credit—or more likely blame—a divine plan for our suffering, we will blame other people. We think that someone else created our misfortune: *It must be due to my family upbringing, my mother or caregiver, my dysfunctional family system, the abandonment I suffered, or the genes that I was born with that were passed on to me by my parents.*

These two explanations for our "problemness"—that they are either random or caused by someone else—can actually coexist. When I was studying at Stanford, I also worked at the Medical Research Institute; the pinnacle of family therapy was developed there. Narrative therapy was also practiced, and we had a narrative clinic. One week, I asked my supervisor during group supervision, "If you have a pair of twins, and one of them becomes a philanthropist and the other one becomes a serial killer, how do you explain that?" In narrative therapy, you don't really look at the psychology of an individual so much as the way the client constructs meaning through social interactions. This is how, as a child develops, they create meaning of experiences.

I said, "How could that make sense? They both grew up together. They received more or less the same social information. Their parental and social experience was constructed in a way that seems not that different."

He said to me, "Oh, well, it's just random."

I was sitting next to a door and I said, "So you mean this doorknob could suddenly just become a flower."

He said, "Yes."

I laughed a little, involuntarily, I was so shocked. I couldn't accept that randomly a doorknob could suddenly become a flower. If that were true, then anything could become anything. We know that's not true. There are laws of cause and effect.

In this way, Buddhism is more like science than religion. We know that scientific law does not ascribe things that happen to some sort of ultimate, superior being. But it also doesn't rest with explanations provided via randomness. Even quantum physics, which has presented us with some very challenging explanations, still breaks everything down to cause and effect on some level. Those materialist scientists are looking for purely physical causes. This is what scientists do as they try to discover the source of a disease, for example. But if you ask a Western scientist, "Why was there an earthquake in Nepal?" their answer may not be very helpful in terms of tackling the problem of suffering.

For example, they may say it happened because of tectonic plates, which does explain things in terms of the conditions that contributed to the event. But it doesn't explain why; only karma does that.

"Why did the earthquake happen?" you might ask a seismologist.

"I just told you why—because of tectonic plates."

"But why were these people killed and those people weren't?"

"It's because their houses were weaker and built near the epicenter."

"But why did it happen in that area, and a few miles away everything was fine?"

When I was getting my degree in clinical psychology and counseling, they told us, "Don't ask your clients 'Why?'" I thought, *But that's the main question*. If one does not understand the causes of a problem, then how does one stop creating them? Karma is the key to understanding why.

Karma Is Mental Energy

It may be helpful to think of karma as mental energy. As human beings, we have five "cameras," related to the five senses, that help us perceive the world. We have the eye camera, the ear camera, the taste camera, the smell camera, and the tactile/touch camera. There is also a sixth, as a sort of hidden camera: the mental camera. When you are dreaming at night, you may not be aware of it, but your mental camera is still operating. Some coma survivors report the same experience. This is how you can see dreams and why you can think about your childhood home when you aren't there.

We experience the world through the five senses, or six, if you count the mind. In fact, there's almost never a time where we are not perceiving something with our senses. You may not be aware when you're walking from your living room to your kitchen. You don't even remember getting there. But there was still a perception going on, an experience happening even if there was also a lack of awareness.

We are probably all familiar with this kind of example; a common one is leaving work and having no recollection of how we drove home. But there is something else even more important that we are also unaware of. Each of our six senses is not only perceiving everything, it is recording everything. It's like you're walking around with a GoPro camera that's filming everything. The camera is going around all day long and storing all of the imprints it receives on a hard drive, which is our consciousness. Each of these imprints is a cause. But another term used for the imprint is *seed*. Seeds germinate, and they produce results. One essential aspect of the law of cause and effect is that karmic seeds are never lost. They are stored in the mind, the consciousness. And it is this consciousness that transmigrates from life to life.

These imprints are countless. Then you start adding up those from previous lives, and it's impossible to perceive the number of imprints you have stored. So where do we even begin? We can start with the fact that imprints have qualities to them, which in turn generate effects. When these effects manifest, the results, one could say, are typically bigger than their causes. There are many elements to karma. For example, it surprised some people to learn that if you didn't create it, you don't experience it. So, in other words, you can't experience the results of your parents' harmful actions since these aren't part of your own mental consciousness. Another interesting thing about karma is that you can create causes. If you have a cause for disease that is strong and ripening already, you can create a cause for health, and sometimes quickly enough to defeat the disease.

One final aspect about karma to mention here is that imprints are never lost until they ripen or are burned away. The beauty of Buddhist practice is we can purify or nullify these imprints so they don't have to ripen. That is a major aspect of our spiritual practice, and the matter to which we will now turn.

About Negative Imprints

Negative imprints necessitate a different way of thinking than many of us are used to. The myth of randomness would have us believe that we can do anything and it doesn't really matter down the line. We might have a basic morality. We know not to go into a store to steal. When we find a wallet, we tend to try to figure out whose it is. I believe that fundamentally humans are good. They are kind, but there is an ignorance at the same time. For many of us, the most philosophical we might get is to say that one should "do unto others as you would have them do unto you." But that is still kind of a mental strategy; it doesn't take into account the process of karmic imprints ripening later in life or even in subsequent lives. If we really believed in cause and effect, we would naturally be very vigilant to not create negative imprints because we'd know we're going to experience the results. Yet the habit is hard to break, of course.

Negative imprints are formed by our behavior. But this has to be understood in the context that imprints are mental, and so it is not the behavior alone (the act of stealing, for example) but the mind that is accompanying that behavior (the greed or disregard for others) that does the imprinting. Just as it is the mind that determines whether certain behavior creates negative, positive, or neutral karma, so it is to the mind we can go to assess whether an imprint is negative, positive, or neutral. Generally speaking, if we're sensitive enough, we'll know if something is a negative imprint because we'll notice it is disturbing our mind. For example, gossiping is considered a negative action. You might say, "Well, I'm just talking to my friends here." But as you develop a calmer and calmer mind and become more sensitive to what is actually upsetting that mind you might find that you instinctively shrink from gossip. That means the action is probably negative, and of course, it also disturbs the minds of others, even if it is subtle. The same can be said for speaking divisively about someone out of jealousy or anger. So much of our political dialogue these days is all about slandering people, it seems; these karmic seeds continue to be planted and ripen in turn.

Negative imprints ripen in the mind like sprouting seeds. This can't be stressed enough. When you're stuck in traffic and someone cuts you off, you start to get agitated. Maybe they start yelling at you, or you start yelling at them. At the very least, you say to yourself, *What's up with that guy?* Throughout this encounter, however, you have a choice about what next step to take. As you develop your awareness, your mindfulness, you can intervene in your habitual way of perceiving things and introduce a healthier and more productive perspective. In other words, you can actually become freer by deciding how to interact with the world rather than follow the usual habitual patterns that keep you bound in the "same old same old," uncontrolled, reactive fabrication.

But when you see the person yelling at you or cutting you off, you might say, "*He's* doing it to me—that angry guy in his big red pickup truck!" We believe that angry guy and the red pickup truck are out there. But where are you experiencing them? In the mind. This is how all the myths flow from the myth of reality. It's not that that guy doesn't exist, but where are you experiencing "that guy"? It's hard to define what in that experience exists *out there*. Because you see his truck cutting in front of you, you see his demeanor and his face, maybe you hear his voice or him honking. But, in fact, we can't see his angry demeanor, the red of his truck, the sound of his horn, without an eye or ear and without a consciousness. There's no experience otherwise. What if we chose to have compassion, thinking that maybe this other person was having a rotten day?

Maybe he was also under the sway of the myth of randomness, so he didn't even know what he was setting himself up for in the future by rudely cutting you off. Or we might even ignore the behavior altogether, in which case it literally ceases to exist—at least for us. So much of our experience with that irate driver is in our minds, isn't it? How we interpret experience is itself due to our karmic imprints. These imprints, again, are stored in our consciousness, and they're experienced in our consciousness even though we think the experience is outside of ourselves. The truck and the guy are just conditions. But the experience is internal, in our mind, in our consciousness.

How Imprints Are Formed

To create a mental imprint, we need four things: intention, an object, an action, and delight or rejoicing in the action. Otherwise, we don't create a full imprint. If you are driving late at night and hit an animal in the road that you didn't see, you do not create negative karma because, first of all, there was no intention, and second, you are likely horrified that you hurt another creature. Without all four of these elements, the imprint is not complete and will not ripen, or if it does ripen, it might be very weak in how it ripens.

If, on the other hand, you have an intention, then you have the makings for a negative karmic imprint. For example, say someone criticizes you and you think, *I really want to hurt his feelings now because I'm upset with him.* Especially because you might feel really happy about following through and hurting his feelings—

because you took delight or rejoiced in that, and are satisfied with what you did—that's a full karmic imprint.

There is a lot to say about each of the four elements of karma, but I think focusing on intention is often the most fruitful for understanding what causes a strong negative imprint to be lodged in one's consciousness. Intention determines the intensity of the result. Let's take a behavior like visiting a prostitute for example. In a traditionally moral system, someone might say that to do so is sexual misconduct, and all sexual misconduct is categorically bad in the same way. But I think we can see how this consensual, if transactional, encounter would carry a different moral weight from other forms of sexual misconduct like sexual assault, or how it would be especially destructive if either individual were already in a committed relationship to someone else.

Now, I'm not advocating any of these behaviors, only pointing out that these actions don't all necessarily carry the same intention as each other. The behaviors are of course abhorrent in real life. But what these examples show is that the weight of the imprints is directly related to the mindset of the person performing the action. The intention has everything to do with the intensity of the karma, as those two words are cognates of each other. And one of the key ways that an intention increases in intensity is through frequency. If you perform a negative behavior a lot, it becomes a habit. The more you do it, the more you enjoy it. In the absence of any opposing power—like regret, or in the Buddhist context, the purification that comes from reciting mantras—the intention is left unchecked, and the karmic results are multiplied. If, on the other hand, you experience regret (the opposite of delight) and take curative actions to counter the negative imprint, you can introduce new, positive imprints that can overpower the other ones. The new imprint doesn't get rid of the old one; that's not the way the mind works. Once the imprint you made before has been made, it's never lost. But you can introduce additional, maybe deeper imprints that lead to increasingly refined states of realization.

Attaining Realization in the Light of Karma

Sometimes we use the word *realization*, which almost sounds synonymous with insight, but it is not. Insights can be very powerful, but are often temporary; realizations never leave you. The best description I've heard is that realizations are what happens when the mind shows some transformation from the inside. Aha moments don't necessarily transform you. That's part of the limitation of therapy; it has power to generate an insight, but that insight doesn't really mean you're going to make the effort necessary to change. The karmic imprints are still leaning too heavily the other way, given our habitual tendencies. With a realization, however, your life begins to change. Even though there will still be work to do, you are never going to go backward.

Let's say you have a realization about impermanence. Then everyday life swoops in and occupies your mind; that realization might be occluded for a time, but when you are in the right position again, your awareness of impermanence will regenerate easily. You have returned to the foundation of that realization, and that foundation will always be yours.

So how do we move from insight into realization? And does that happen suddenly or gradually? In our present society, it is common to be enthralled with whatever is dramatic and/or easy, so we naturally prefer the notion of sudden enlightenment. Yet from the perspective of the myth we are presently discussing, the notion of instantaneous enlightenment or instant realization appears as both a romantic and an illogical concept. And this is because it makes it seem as if it is an experience that happens randomly and without cause. If such a sudden awakening was causeless, then it could happen at any time to anyone, whether they are a spiritual adept or not. In addition, we couldn't work toward such a goal; rather, we'd just have to wait around until it happened, rather than putting any effort into the undertaking. This is a clear example of the type of thinking exhibited when we're under the influence of the myth of randomness.

Rather, what the law of karma teaches us is that all events must have a cause. And these causes must be created. And if they are created, then there must be a gradual unfolding of cause and effect. Otherwise, if the cause for enlightenment was to, say, meditate on your forehead, then the meditator should immediately experience the result of sudden enlightenment. Obviously, while one's experience of realization is a causal event, it is dependent upon a multitude of causes and conditions. And these causes must be created by the adept—likely cultivated over a length of time—or there will never be the experience of realization, sudden or otherwise.

The process of attaining insight into emptiness—that is, into reality—is therefore a calculated one. When a person has direct insight into reality, it can be perceived as something that happens suddenly, especially if one is only focusing on the few moments of the transition from ignorance to awakening into that experience. We hear stories about the adepts who attained enlightenment when their teacher slapped them with his sandal, or while emptying their teacher's bedpan, or in the moment a candle is blown out. In truth, however, attaining realization is more similar to the action of turning on a light. We could assume the light went on instantly, but a light going on is anything but instant. There are a multitude of causes and conditions associated with that seemingly single act of switching on the light. There are all the people involved in the construction of the house—the architect, the framer, the plumber, the electrician, the roofer, and so on—all of those people are needed to be able to turn on a light in a dark room. We can even trace the ability to turn on a light back to the inventors of the light bulb. There's a whole Wikipedia page devoted to how electric light came into creation. Someone needed to figure out how to shape the glass, affix it to a base that could receive the electricity, find a conductor and filament, and so forth. Then, for light to reach us today, power plants were envisioned and constructed, and the wiring from the power plant to the neighborhood was laid over several miles. Then the wiring had to be connected to your house. The switch was installed on your wall, and the light sockets or wall outlets needed configuring. Then you walked across the room and touched a switch, seven steps that were also a result of a complex series of causes, and you turned on the switch and said, "Aha! The light turned on instantly!"

A single "instantaneous act"? It takes ages for that

"instant" to happen. A sudden moment of realization of profound truth is exactly the same.

Understanding Karma Does Not Condone Bad Behavior

Before we close this chapter, I would like to return to the earlier point about how every event takes place in the mind. Many years ago, I heard of a study performed in the Tibetan refugee communities in India. What was unknown to much of the modern world until fairly recently was the unspeakable torture that tens of thousands of Tibetans suffered at the hands of the Chinese occupiers of Tibet. We are well aware of the killing fields of Cambodia, the atrocities in Uganda, and the horrific history of the Holocaust. But if you read accurate accounts of what the Chinese occupiers did, have done, and are still doing to the Tibetan population they invaded, it would bring tears to your eyes. You might even doubt that human beings could treat their fellow human beings so horribly, subjecting them to the absolute worst torture techniques one can think of.

So a group of psychologists set out on an eight-month research project to study the effects of torture among the refugees who had been imprisoned in Chinese prison camps in Tibet. Specifically, they were studying the effects of trauma from torture. Now, these refugees did suffer varying degrees of post-traumatic stress disorder. But seemingly the effects were significantly lower than would be expected, and that was curious to the researchers. What they discovered was that the victims' use of their spiritual practice, which was natural for their culture, had a direct effect on the severity of their PTSD. Most of these subjects also attended Western psychotherapy, and while accepting that these methods may have helped them some, they nonetheless thought these interventions were quite crude.

Some of the researchers were curious about how trauma could have this lower level of impact on their Tibetan subjects, so they asked the Dalai Lama if he had any theories on this. His Holiness replied that he believed there were possibly two factors involved in the lower indicators of PTSD, the symptoms of which include nightmares, heightened anxiety, self-destructive behavior, insomnia, and so forth. First, he pointed out that as a culture, the concept of karma—the law of cause and effect—is embedded strongly from a very early age. Now, an understanding of karma does not condone bad behavior. Bad behavior is wrong for no other reason than it causes suffering to another person—and to the torturer themself, as their actions plant seeds, or karmic imprints, on their own continuum that will cause them to suffer similarly, perhaps worse, in the future. But His Holiness said that even uneducated Tibetans accept the law of karma and thus take some of the blame for their own experience. By "blame," I really mean accountability. Culturally, they just naturally accept that they come into this life with their own set of "mental DNA," meaning that the consciousness that takes rebirth is not a tabula rasa, a blank slate. But instead, depending on actions that leave imprints in previous lives, the mind has its own unique set of imprints that can ripen when the conditions present themselves. If the person, in this case one of the Tibetan victims we are referring to, has a basic belief in the laws of cause and effect, then they can appreciate on some level that their Chinese tormentors are more the *conditions* of their agony rather than the fundamental cause. This understanding does create a different meaning around their experience. So while the pain these victims experienced would be the same as anyone, the narratives they generated about the abuse may be different. Of course, the people who were tortured experienced severe pain and were even angry at their torturers, but with the added understanding of karma, they were probably less vengeful. The degree that a victim thought this way was, of course, highly variable. They may generate a sense of regret—not guilt—that they too had a hand in creating the circumstances they found themselves in, and perhaps they could even feel a sense of relief that the karmic imprints they created were now extinguished. However, this is considered quite an advanced way of thinking, though it is not impossible. An advanced practitioner would not want to recreate further negative imprints by generating hateful and revengeful thoughts. I understand what I'm presuming here may sound unrealistic for most of us, but it is important, I feel, to present an alternative to our "normal" and habitual manner of reacting. I also understand this is an extreme example, but perhaps it will make us more hopeful that we can transform our own difficulties, which are hopefully much less intense in nature.

His Holiness then commented that in some rare instances, as in the cases of highly realized spiritual adepts, they not only recognized the ripening of karma in the abuse they endured, but they would also—and this may be hard to believe—generate compassion toward their abusers. In the Buddhist teachings, we are taught that developing profound wisdom must be balanced with developing great compassion. There are numerous teachings and practices that urge us to generate compassion toward our enemies, for the benefits are great; the harder it is to develop compassion toward an object, the more the compassion will strengthen within our mindstream. Because Buddhism is a vehicle for mental health, compassion is seen as one of the key practices and mental attitudes to develop for our own, and others, happiness. Perhaps Jesus was one of the greatest examples of this truth: even on the cross he did not waver in his commitment to compassion, but rather said, "Oh Father, forgive them for they know not what they do."

5
The Myth of Happiness

One day I was playing golf with another member of my club, Crazy Bennie, as he was known—a nickname garnered during his days as the owner of fine audio equipment for automobiles. The golf course is ranked as the fourteenth best course in the country and is semiprivate, meaning it is also open to the public for play. I was a new member, and Bennie and I occasionally played together as he was friendly to newcomers like me. He was an older gentleman, retired, single . . . and a bit frugal.

As Bennie and I were walking down the twelfth fairway, he turned to me and said, "You know, I read your book."

He was referring to my first book, *The Misleading Mind*. I was a bit shocked, as Bennie seemed to only be interested in golf, watching sports on TV, and discussing conservative politics.

I said to him, "Really? I'm a surprised you bought it."

He replied, "Oh, I didn't buy it. You just go onto Amazon and where it says, 'Look inside this book,' I read it there."

I commented that the whole book was not available to read that way, but he responded by saying he could read every other page for a few chapters and he got the basic premise. Then he said, "You know, what is it with you Buddhists? It's always about suffering. But I'm not suffering. I'm happy! I belong to a beautiful golf course and play whenever I want. I don't have a wife making demands on me." (He'd been divorced twice.) "I eat when and what I want, then I settle down to a scotch in the evening as I watch the latest game."

I felt disheartened. I had clearly failed to explain in *The Misleading Mind* the nature of suffering in a way he could understand, or maybe the pages Amazon provided were just missing the essential points.

As we proceeded to the green, he started to complain about the slow group ahead that was blocking us; he was afraid he was going to lose the rhythm of his stroke. Then he commented on how the greenskeeper was keeping these greens too slow. He switched over to expressing intense frustration with the president and the liberal politics that were destroying the country. Next, I heard about how the water had been shut off in his neighborhood, and he hadn't had water for two days—it was a real pain that some stupid maintenance worker had broken the main water line. Finally, the group ahead of us started to move toward the thirteenth hole and our play could resume—but not before I heard about his health problems: issues with his eyes that were affecting his sight, a loss of energy as he grew older, and other maladies. *Hmm*, I thought, *at least he isn't suffering!* But I kept my thoughts to myself.

There is little reason to engage in the Buddhist

approach to mental health if we lack the understanding and appreciation of what a Buddhist is referring to when bringing up the topic of suffering. We discussed some alternatives to the word *suffering* itself in the introduction, when I proposed "dissatisfactoriness" or "problemness" to help provide different shades of meaning to the term. I did so because I believe that the word *suffering* in English does not nearly capture the meaning as it is explained in the original Buddhist languages of Sanskrit or Pali, or even later in Tibetan. I think when English speakers use the word *suffering*, their mental image is of people being bombed in Ukraine or starving in a poor African country or experiencing homelessness on the streets in the US. Or it might be more personal than that, such as a friend struggling with cancer, but conceptions of suffering are all pretty much confined to a physical situation. And while these are certainly conditions of suffering, they do not nearly capture the broad scope of the concept of suffering as the Buddha originally taught it. This topic is complex and deep, but without some understanding and appreciation of the principle, there is not really much basis for engaging with it in an authentic way or with the philosophy and practices explained in Buddhism.

Happiness vs. Suffering

I'll see if I can help unpack this essential topic, although it is very difficult and I'm not sure I'll do a good job. But then again, the Buddha himself was unsure he could do a good job. After attaining enlightenment under the Bodhi Tree in India, a state of nirvana where he would no long ever experience unhappiness, he remained silent for seven weeks. He felt there was no way he could communicate this state of ultimate satisfaction to others. They just wouldn't get it. Finally, after being convinced by both celestial beings and human beings that he should teach what he had discovered, he relented. And isn't it interesting that his very first teaching was on the nature of suffering: that all beings are oppressed and not free. They are not liberated, rather they are imprisoned by various afflictions and mental disorders, and they don't even know it!

In my early days of being immersed in the Buddhist tradition, I wondered why he didn't start with the third noble truth, the release from suffering—which is the state of ultimate peace and satisfaction, nirvana—rather than starting with suffering itself. This certainly would make for an easier, prepackaged sell in the modern Western world! Over the years, as I have considered this, I have come to understand that the Buddha made great effort to educate us about suffering first because if we don't know what suffering really is, then, we can assume, our idea of happiness would be similarly skewed.

It's strange to think that we don't know what happiness is when, fundamentally, all we are doing is seeking some sort of experience to feel better. This in itself gives us a clue into what is meant by suffering, and especially into its all-pervasiveness. For if we are always seeking to feel better or seeking to maintain the good feeling we have or trying to avoid an unpleasant experience, then, logically speaking, we are not secure in our happiness. in fact, we are in a constant state of dis-ease. Our "happiness" is always in danger of evaporating in the very next moment.

And further, what we are calling happiness, when further analyzed, tends to be equated with a feeling of pleasure or pleasantness. This kind of tentativeness around our feelings and positive experiences clearly implies that we are constantly on shaky ground—merely trying to stave off the next unpleasant experience or prolong a pleasant one. This is a big part of what is meant by the Buddhist notion of suffering: we are not relaxed in our own skin or in our own mind, as a baseline. When our contentment, good feelings, happiness, and satisfaction are by nature fleeting, then is that real happiness? Bouncing around from one good feeling to the next is not the Buddhist idea of happiness or contentment. That is a constant sense of anxiety that demands we stay vigilant about keeping the feel-good experience happening and avoiding the loss of it. The loss of that feel-good experience is a state that is not pleasant, yet that really is our baseline. If this is the case—that we have to constantly keep moving toward pleasure to avoid the unpleasant—then we can say our general state of being is unpleasantness. This unpleasantness may be just below the surface, but the point remains. We cannot claim to be happy when we are constantly trying to seek or maintain a feeling of contentment and well-being.

One could argue, if our unhappiness lies below the surface even as it is directing our moment-to-moment thoughts, feelings, and activities, "But isn't ignorance bliss?" This "ignorance is bliss" argument is a bit like thinking that since dogs love dog food, then we should all just remain ignorant and settle for dog food, too. From the Buddhist practitioner's point of view, having seen the potential for great joy and happiness, mundane pleasures appear like dog food. Most of us have eaten great meals; we would never give up those fortunate dining experiences to settle for dog food. By the same token, neither would the spiritual person settle for mundane, ephemeral, fleeting pleasures in exchange for the state of liberation from all mental anguish, afflictions, and disorders. If you can have filet mignon, why eat a can of Alpo?

Yet we resist coming to the realization that things in life are actually difficult, painful, and dissatisfying and that our pursuit to numb this through pleasures seems, well, pretty unreal. For example, you may have noticed that you can't stay in one place for very long. You get hungry, so you sit down for a meal, and then you need to get up when you're finished. You may go to the couch to watch TV, but after a while get tired and go to bed. If you found happiness in bed, then why do you get up in the morning? If your job made you happy, then why not stay at work all the time? If taking a vacation were true happiness, what would it be like if you stayed on holiday all the time?

I knew people who thought that being on holiday was the key to happiness. They made enough money so that they could go on a cruise every year. First they went for a month. Then three months. Then six months. Yet they were no happier than anyone else. When they were on the ship, they'd complain that the quality of the food had deteriorated, the entertainment consisted of the same old shows, and they'd been to most of the ports of call so they would not go ashore. They contemplated switching alliances to another cruise line as they heard the other line had more interesting ports and more restaurants. But then they found out the ship was too large with too many passengers—less intimate. Where does the search for happiness end? This is what the Buddha was trying to tell us when he said we are in the nature of suffering. Suffering is not the cruise line. Suffering is in the mind.

This is of course a depressing thought when there is nothing to replace this difficult situation. If we try to find a suitable antidote for suffering, we find that the opposite of that concept is not exactly happiness, although happiness is a byproduct. The absence of suffering means there is wisdom—the wisdom of knowing how things exist and how we exist as well. In that state of wisdom, everything appears as soft, gentle, nonthreatening, peaceful, and clear. The byproduct of this is we are possessed by a mind that is so balanced and unagitated that the natural effect is happiness, but a happiness that is unusual in the sense that we don't ever experience it, because it is nondiminishing—it doesn't fade or morph into some new agitated, unfulfilled state of mind. Thus, the actual opposite of suffering is awakening. This distinction in Buddhist thought is highly relevant. Awakening, or awakened buddhahood, is the ultimate state of happiness, which never diminishes.

The Definition of Happiness

So if happiness isn't the opposite of suffering, yet we pursue happiness with everything we are worth, why do we do this? What is our "definition" of happiness that will allow us to know if we possess it? I find it strange that modern psychology, whose chief goal appears to be the pursuit of happiness, almost entirely defines it as feeling bad less. That is what the entire discipline is focused on.

Don't believe me? Consider the Diagnostic and Statistical Manual 5 (DSM-5), which is the official reference that mental health professionals use in assessing mental health conditions. When therapists submit insurance claims, they will need to provide a diagnosis from this manual. There are 297 primary diagnoses with numerous subvariants. These diagnoses will typically provide the foundation for developing a treatment plan for the client. There are twenty-one broad categories in which an individual diagnosis may fall. Some of the broad categories found in the manual are dissociative disorders, anxiety disorders, depressive disorders, psychotic disorders, neurodevelopmental disorders (ADHD, autism spectrum), and so on. When I was studying for my master's in psychology, we studied all of these diagnoses over a one-year period. It was a common occurrence among the students that whatever category of disorders we were studying at the time, everyone would walk away feeling they had that disorder. When studying depressive disorders, we would think, "Ah! So that's what's wrong with me! I have persistent depressive disorder!" Then a week or two later, studying anxiety disorders, we would self-diagnose as having separation anxiety disorder or any one (or all) of the other anxiety disorders, like panic attack, social anxiety disorder, and so on.

It could get, well, depressing. And perhaps the most depressing part about it, the thing that struck me was that in this manual, and in the various theories I studied, there was no clear definition of happiness. In other words, all these problems were in juxtaposition to . . .

what? What was the endgame? The goal for overcoming these disorders through the intervention offered by psychotherapy, be it happiness, contentment, satisfaction, or balance, was stated but never clearly defined. And while there may have been a few attempts by various experts to give some sort of definition of happiness, these experts rarely agreed with each other. This is in stark contrast to a Buddhist practitioner, whether they follow Tibetan Buddhism, Theravada, Zen, Chan, or any other form of Buddhism. They will all agree on the goal and definition of happiness: the actualization of one's true nature of clarity, a state that is cultivated by ridding the mind of the clouds of afflictions, delusions, and emotional toxins—also known as nirvana, liberation, enlightenment, or awakening.

Happiness Is Not Pleasure

Without a clear goal of what we are trying to obtain in our pursuit of happiness, what we are left with instead is the myth of happiness. In that myth, the idea of happiness and the pursuit of pleasure are synonymous. The formula is simple: more pleasure equals more happiness. Or, more comfort equals more contentment. Our culture is obsessed not only with increasing the degree of pleasure but in having it last longer. More cable channels mean more viewing pleasure, of a greater duration and variety. We are flooded with the societal pressure to meet the right partner, and yet how long does the honeymoon period really last? We think, *I'll really be satisfied if I can go out for sushi tonight*. But how long does that "happiness" last? Many of us are fortunate to have material comfort and security; this is good. But clinging to the things that bring comfort and the idea that we need to continually feed our own comfort needs, and even increase them—that is flawed.

We pursue pleasure—and therefore "happiness"—in things that are inherently incapable of providing anything more than a limited high. If drinking a good bottle of wine were really happiness, then why couldn't we just keep drinking and experience more happiness? The problem is not in these objects outside ourselves. This misguided and ignorant thinking that happiness comes from pleasure, or the avoidance of discomfort, only creates a life that ends meaningless and unfulfilled. Not only are we seeking a level of pleasure that brings no fulfillment, we also believe the objects we seek out are inherently pleasing.

My teacher Lama Yeshe would travel to the West annually. Upon returning to Nepal, he would say to me, "I am so sad in the West because people there are suffering much more than the people here. Sure, they have such material success, but they are miserable inside. The people here are very simple. Poor. But they are much more content."

In the West, we seek happiness through an incredible variety of sources—a loving relationship, getting or being in shape, getting high or buzzed, sleeping in late, hanging out with our children or grandchildren, sex, good food, a good career with good income—but we never experience true and lasting happiness. This is even written into the US Declaration of Independence: there it is the "pursuit" of happiness, not the experience of happiness, that we are guaranteed a right to.

And the pursuit of happiness is actually the pursuit of pleasure—first one, and then another. If we stick with any one pleasure long enough, we get bored with it, or it becomes ordinary and mundane. Even sex, which some consider the highest and purest form of pleasure, turns to suffering. If not, then having constant sex would provide constant happiness; so why does the experience wane? If you think of any one single pleasure you enjoy, if you analyze carefully, you can see that really there is no essence of pleasure or happiness in the object. Everything, given enough time, will turn into a problem. If happiness were in a slice of cheesecake, then it should always offer contentment. If that were true, then the fifth slice of cheesecake you eat would bring you the same happiness as the first bite.

Some people have wised up to the fact that this kind of pleasure-seeking does not produce lasting results, nor does it give the feeling of having arrived at a final, contented destination. They do not want to pursue happiness, they want to have already arrived to a state of happiness. These people may turn to a particular shade of happiness that carries a feeling of permanence: security. They believe the primary purpose of life is to be secure in one's health, relationships, and resources: a sort of freedom from fear and anxiety.

Is the real, deep meaning of life to just survive with comfort? I am not questioning the importance of meeting basic human needs; those are essential for everyone. I am saying the "cult of more" leads us into disarray and dissatisfaction, like drinking salt water to quench our thirst. It is said that once a person makes enough income to have a house and fulfill basic needs, their level of happiness does not increase with added income. In other words, we need our security, health, and resources, but extra luxury does not provide more happiness. What does? A sense of purpose and connection with others, which arises, in part, from an appreciation of impermanence and change and the pursuit of awakening one's true potential.

Lama Yeshe used to say, "You people don't even know how to enjoy a cup of tea. You ruin it by not simply enjoying the experience but by grasping and clinging for it to last forever." As soon as the enjoyment from the tea fades, we pour another cup with the hope of extending the enjoyment. But the next one is never as good as the first. The tea has already begun to cool in the pot. Recently I bought a mug that keeps my coffee piping hot for an hour and a half. Then I started investigating one that can keep it hot for four hours. With respect to pleasure and enjoyment, we are like addicts constantly trying to maintain our high. The problem is not the cooling of the tea. The problem is in my grasping for it to stay hot, because more pleasure means more happiness . . . or does it?

We Are Entitled to Real Happiness

In Western civilization, we discuss the "meaning of life" as an existential question. The particulars of that question are often left up to philosophers, theorists, psychologists, and the like. By contrast, Buddhists, even those who ascribe to Buddhism as a cultural identity rather than chiefly as a spiritual path, share a common knowledge as to what the meaning of life is: the meaning of life is to be happy. All actions, pursuits, and intentions of any living being are the same: the achievement of happiness and contentment. This applies to the baby crying out for its parent's comfort, the homeless person asking for help, the businessperson who is trying to provide a good life for their family. The pursuit of happiness is really no different for the squirrel alertly looking for acorns while at the same time paying attention to its surroundings to avoid being killed by a predator on the ground or in the air. Even the tiny ant will avert danger if it senses it. While we may not automatically translate these actions as the pursuit of happiness, they are indeed just that; whether it's to preserve one's life, experience the joy of a child's contentment, or create a successful business. We undertake all these things in the pursuit of happiness—even breathing one breath to the next (think of the distress or even panic one experiences the very moment our breathing becomes obstructed). We are unmistakably driven to either experience pleasure or avoid pain and distress.

Buddhist thought insists we are entitled to real happiness. We all have buddha nature, which is the unrealized potential for full awakening that every living being possesses. But this potential is not like some little buddha sitting inside of us somewhere, waiting to be discovered and set free. It is a potential that is an actual quality of our mind. It's like a piece of marble that has the potential to be carved into a David. But the David doesn't exist in the marble already. It has to be actualized through the creative vision of the sculptor, Michelangelo.

We're entitled to happiness, but the problem is that what we typically believe to be happiness and the pathway to real happiness are the exact opposite. There is no happiness in experiencing disturbing emotions or afflictive minds, not at the beginning, in the middle, or at the end. The more adept and experienced the practitioner, the earlier and earlier they will intervene in the pursuit of this false happiness so that real happiness may be pursued. And they view us with compassion as our efforts fail to grasp and realize the happiness we are seeking.

It is like the person who has dementia. They do not remember who you are or think you're someone else, and you feel a sense of sadness. You would not wish that mindset on anyone. My mother suffered from Alzheimer's disease; when she broke her hip and was in the hospital, she pleaded with my sister to get her out of there, telling her, "The baby is not due yet." It was, I must admit, a little comical at first, but mostly it was heartbreaking. The awakened, or awakening, Buddhist sees that we all are in a state of dementia—we are all mistaken about our circumstances. The world we see is not the world that is described by the sages: like a dream that we believe is real. What follows next is a feeling of intense compassion for living beings and a spontaneous urge to do something to help them. Through a wise and compassionate attitude, their actions, words, and presence can be of the utmost benefit to the suffering of others.

There is such a thing as a lasting, nondiminishing, eternal happiness. This is not only the meaning of life, but it is the meaning of all our lives into the future. And it is attainable, provided we generate a strong conviction to pursue it. But if we don't know what is possible, and how great our potential is, then we will stay caught in some low-level quality of life, thinking we're happy when all we're doing is trying to maintain pleasantness and security. We are just treading water until we become exhausted. In the background of our restlessness, we sense that pleasantness and security are short-lived. We know the pleasant feeling is going to end, and we know our kids are going to grow up and move out. We know we're going to have to retire and change our lifestyle. We know we are going to die. So we try continuously to maintain the pleasure, the security, and the warmth. This endless requirement of maintenance, and the self-absorption it thrives on, is considered suffering.

Self-Cherishing

A common modern-day belief is that to be happy we have to make ourselves happy. We have to look out for number one. Philosophically and psychologically, this is the exact opposite of what truly leads to a happy, fulfilled person. The belief in focusing on oneself first has become more and more prevalent in our culture and is echoed in many therapeutic approaches. Some will use that quote from the flight attendant before takeoff to "put your own oxygen mask on before assisting others" as an example of this me-first value. By contrast, truly compassionate people demonstrate that an "other-first" focus is the best technique for self-fulfillment and happiness. To be clear, we are not talking about martyrdom here; the purpose of life is to be happy, after all. It is the thinking and methodology behind happiness we want to question and investigate. That all unhappiness is the result of self-cherishing or "self-first" behavior needs to be thoroughly researched and reflected upon. Buddhists believe that the focus upon solely one's own happiness is not only flawed as a remedy to unhappiness, lack of fulfillment, and lasting contentment; further, the one common denominator in all of our strife is this clinging to "I," "me," and "mine."

On the other hand, compassion for others not only makes the world a happier place but, strangely, makes the person practicing compassion happier as well. It is simple to see in daily life: when we act and think in a truly compassionate way, we take ourselves out of our self-pitying, depressed attitude and that makes us happier. When we practice compassion, we can tame, strengthen, and enlighten the mind to the point where it understands that it alone can ward off any threat to its happiness. And the main practice to do this is to cherish others more than oneself.

In this context, allow me to recount the story of Atisha here. Atisha was a renowned Indian scholar and practitioner during the eleventh century. When Tibet's religious tradition had fallen into disrepair following a period of political turmoil—not unlike the turmoil Tibet has endured for the past sixty-plus years—the new king of the time asked Atisha to help reestablish Buddhism in the kingdom. Atisha agreed; he ended up traveling to Tibet and remained there until his passing some seventeen years later.

Once when Atisha was circumambulating a holy site in Lhasa, the capital of Tibet, as he walked he encountered a person reciting prayers outside the temple. Atisha said to him, "It's very good to recite prayers, but it would be better if you practiced Dharma!" Here, *Dharma* means the spiritual path as Buddhism describes it.

The next day, Atisha was again at the temple circumambulating when he saw this same man, who was now circumambulating along with him. Atisha said to the fellow, "It's very good to be circumambulating, but it would be better if you practiced Dharma!"

The following day, Atisha was again outside the temple circumambulating when he encountered the same man, who this time was engaged in meditation. Atisha interrupted the poor fellow only to admonish him by saying, "It's good to practice meditation, but it'd be better to practice Dharma!"

By now, the man had had enough. He shouted out, "I'm trying to practice the spiritual path! What am I doing wrong? What do you mean by 'practice Dharma'?"

To this, Atisha calmly replied, "Give up doing these activities merely for the sake of this life, this momentary happiness only."

So we see, what Atisha was harping on was this guy's motivation for engaging in those "spiritual activities." He detected the man was in it merely for the pursuit of short-term fulfillment. Spiritual practice, training the mind, is not judged from the activity one engages in, but from the mindset, the motivation, by which one engages in it. There is no need to put on robes, live in a monastery or hermitage, or take on some other outwardly "spiritual" or religious form to practice the Dharma. It is the mind that determines whether or not one is engaged in spiritual development.

It is well-known in the Buddhist tradition that some of the most accomplished spiritual adepts appear humble and unassuming. One cannot judge from outward appearances whether or not a person is spiritual. Personally, I can report that among the most advanced practitioners I've ever met, you would hardly notice their having any spiritual attainments at all—until you hang around them long enough. Then their qualities will seep out, and eventually it is as if you can "smell" the aroma of their realizations. Further, we actually have a belief that if someone talks about their realizations, we should walk away. A person's realizations or attainments should speak for themselves in that person's behavior, demeanor, and personality. Any declaration of one's spiritual attainments has no intention other than to enhance the person's reputation or status—in other words, it is ego embellishment for the benefit of the person and not for the living beings they are supposed to be putting first. It's just an ego trip.

For our purposes here, Atisha aptly described the myth of happiness when he criticized someone for seeking the happiness of only this life. That is short-term happiness, which you have seen is not happiness at all. The pursuit of this short-term happiness can be fairly easily detected. In Buddhist thought there are eight considerations by which it is evaluated, and they are presented in pairs of opposites. We are engaging in seeking short-term happiness if we are seeking pleasure and avoiding pain; if we are seeking praise and avoiding blame; if we are seeking fame and avoiding unimportance; and if we are seeking gain and avoiding loss.

The Purpose of the Guru Is to Insult You

The list of dualities of mundane concerns—pleasure and pain, praise and blame, and so on—may seem very clear, and intellectually we might appreciate how either side of a particular dichotomy interferes with our progress on the spiritual path. We also likely understand that avoiding these dualities can be tricky at best. In fact, it can be quite difficult. I can relate.

Lama Yeshe once asked me to help run the finances for the monastery. Each evening, I would sit down with the acting abbot, Lama Lhundrup, and the manager, Lama Pasang, for a "money meeting." It was kind of hilarious because I knew nothing about bookkeeping and was rather a failure at math in general. As for Lama Lhundrup and Lama Pasang, while they were sort of innately adept at business, they were lifetime monks who had taken vows not to engage in such worldly matters. But, if nothing else, Tibetans, including monastics, are practical.

Our meetings would last an hour or two and were structured around Lama Pasang's daily shopping duty. During monsoon season he often could not reach Kathmandu, as our road would become a stream; this also meant that with all the rain there was less food available in the bazaar. Perhaps it was due to these challenges that when Lama Pasang left the monastery with 5,000 rupees, he would inevitably only be able later to account for 4,923 or 5,201. Never 5,000. His accounting would be based on his memory with some receipts thrown in here and there.

For most of the year, Lama Yeshe was traveling, often teaching abroad. But when he came back to Kopan

Monastery, his home, he went through everything, and I mean, everything, with a fine-tooth comb. He especially wanted to know about the finances. He was adamant that every rupee be accounted for. He drummed into us over and over again that handling "Dharma" money was not the same as handling business money. Money given to the monastery on behalf of supporting the monks and nuns or for other religious purposes had to be spent ethically and for the monastery's needs only. No waste. No personal benefit. No salaries. Wages to workers had to be at the low end of the scale, while still being fair. Lama was highly meticulous because it is considered very negative karma to waste money that is raised for Dharma purposes. There is not much room to use money donated for religious purposes on items or for purposes that are considered luxuries or enjoyment, unless it was donated for that reason.

One night while we were having our money meeting, Lama Yeshe came into the office. He had the air of a tall lawman entering a saloon. Lama Pasang knew what was coming and silently slipped behind Lama and out of the office. Lama Lhundrup and I were trapped behind the desk. Lama started going through every drawer and file cabinet, collecting loose pieces of paper and receipts that were five years old and illegible. He would ask what they were, had they been paid, was what we spent fair, and other questions for which there were no real answers.

"You spent 5,347 rupees on milk. How many pounds was that?" The receipt of course was in kilos.

"I don't know, Lama."

"What! You're an American college-educated boy and

you don't know how much milk each of my children get a week?"

Digital calculators had just been invented, but any attempt to do the math was no use. "Here it says you spent 453 rupees on cooking oil. How many tins was that? Why isn't it written here?"

The grilling was like having a root canal without anesthetic. It went on for an hour or two. I had a low fever. I had not had dinner. It was getting on to ten o'clock at night. It was raining outside. Finally, when he left, I just sort of broke down. I'd had it.

Now, this was not an unusual event. A great lama once said, "The purpose of the guru is to insult you." That may sound like a guru should be abusive—it is anything but that. If you are committed to subduing your self-centered attitude and you have a real relationship with an authentic teacher who has no self-interest but only other-interest, then "tough love" can be the best way to go. But this is based on an agreement between the teacher and the student, otherwise there can be too much of a power imbalance. The lama cannot have ego. The student must have confidence and trust in the teacher.

As I was outside in the light rain, I saw that the light was still on in the kitchen. I knew I should eat something, and I knew the cook would look after me. So I went into the kitchen through the back door, and before I could stop myself, I saw Lama Yeshe standing there with the cook. They both looked at me. It was just the three of us in the smoky atmosphere of the kitchen—we cooked on wood then, for all hundred or so monks. I froze thinking how I could get away. I had nothing left and didn't want more stern discipline.

Lama looked at me and said, "Something?"

I don't remember saying anything, and then he said, "What?! You need to hear 'I love you'?"

I don't think he was telling me he loved me, which I knew he did. He was asking me if I was feeling so sad for myself that I needed to know someone loved me. It was part mocking and part deep compassion, if the two can coexist. He was mocking my ego but so skillfully teaching me that I could leave my need for praise behind, and thus the futile need to try and comfort my ego. This event had a profound effect on me, and I still resonate with it today. It let me know that we are all looking for love, but to be dependent upon it is a depressant. One doesn't feel more love by wallowing in the self-pitying attitude that no one loves you or the idea that you just need more love from others. This may sound cold, but I'm bringing it up in the context of what really brings lasting happiness. It comes from cherishing others as much as yourself. And the great saints cherish others more than themselves.

Make no mistake, though. The reason to cherish others' happiness is somewhat selfish, or as His Holiness the Dalai Lama says, it is "wise selfishness." Overly focusing on one's own happiness does not lead to happiness, but focusing on others' happiness may make them happy and will certainly make yourself happier—if done correctly and not out of martyrdom or unhealthy codependence.

We Can Get There Over Time

An important takeaway about the myth of happiness is to understand that the cause of happiness, which we all strive for in every moment of our existence, is not to eradicate all the discomforts and harms of the outer world. That would be an endless and fruitless endeavor. It just does not work. The eighth-century scholar and meditator Shantideva famously said that the fool tries to cover the world with leather in order to eliminate the pain of stepping on a thorn; the wise man takes a small piece of leather and covers his foot with a sandal.

Since we are dealing with the most important purpose in the universe, your happiness, it is vital to understand the formula for achieving and accessing a level of happiness and fulfillment that is beyond our daily grasp . . . but *is* within our grasp to achieve over time. And it is not just the goal of achieving this ultimate fulfillment that is our only purpose. The very act of working toward it, the "path," is one that leads increasingly, incrementally, to more and more fulfillment. It's a gradual process that has the benefit of fulfilling the needs of others in its wake, or at least improving their lives in even small ways.

The myth of happiness has been about self-directed, short-term happiness. There is, however, a happiness that is enduring, a happiness that is deeper. This happiness has qualities that are exultant. The happiness we're talking about here is the buddha nature that we possess, a potential that is always within us that is a lot more deeply satisfying than the happiness most of us typically settle for. Buddha nature can be described as a fully awakened state of consciousness. We all possess buddha nature, though this transcendental state of mind is presently undeveloped within us. To develop that fully is a lofty goal, perhaps, but even in the process of developing it, we gain more control over our neurotic minds.

This potential mind exists within every person; we can all awaken to a happiness that is nondiminishing and eternal, in the sense that it keeps on giving.

We have seen here that, contrary to popular belief, the more self-concerned a person is, the less they are able to meet their need for happiness. Happiness arises instead from a sense of commonality, care, and connection. Empathy, love, and compassion are the actual antidotes to depression, isolation, and self-loathing—our roadblocks to true satisfaction.

6
The Myth of Only Living Once

Throughout this book you have likely been able to glimpse my agenda. I feel that a number of Buddhist writers and teachers today are oversimplifying the rich tradition of Buddhist thought. They are trying to please their audience, and they do this in part by not presenting ideas that are provocative or difficult. I refuse to be one of those people. Of course, it is the modern Buddhist writer's job to translate the material into present-day parlance. But we should do so only so that people can consider whether these ideas are true or not. The goal should not be to change the core ideas in the hope that they will be at least partially adopted.

There is a seventh-century document called the *Sixteen Guidelines* (sometimes 16G for short), which were a set of ethics presented by the king of Tibet before Buddhism took a very strong foothold there. These guidelines played a big role in the transformation of Tibet into a peaceful civilization. Lama Zopa Rinpoche thought these guidelines about how to live your life in a more ethical way were a good jumping-off point to the ideas of Buddhism for modern, non-Buddhist people. So our organization translated those verses and then gave some commentary by Lama Zopa.

When the translation was complete, Lama Zopa asked me and two senior students, one an accomplished editor and the other a translator, to go through this book with him, which consisted of guidelines in sixteen verses. We went through it for ten nights, every evening, from about eleven at night until three in the morning. Sometimes I'd look over and John would be nodding off . . . but overall it was a powerful experience. We went through all sixteen of the guidelines as well as the commentary and the explanation that was given in the book that they produced. On balance, however, Lama Zopa wasn't very happy with what the translators had done. He found their approach to be overly compensative for nonbelievers, as the editors tried to imagine what some of the objections might be and then curtail the work accordingly.

One verse had a reference to reincarnation. Each verse was short, just four lines; that's how it was written. So taking out a big piece from any verse was immediately obvious. In that translation of this verse, the reference to reincarnation was completely left out.

The modern version of verse 10 read:

> Know how to enjoy food and wealth without falling to
> the two extremes of extravagance and deprivation.

But in the actual text, the verse was composed like this:

Since food and wealth depend upon the
power of past generosity,
though you take great care looking after
all you've amassed,
still you can't be sure it will increase.
If you want to add to the happiness
and well-being of this and future lives,
use what prosperity you have towards
offerings and aid.

Lama Zopa was upset. Shaking his head, he asked, "Why? Why would they take 'future lives' out?"

We explained that reincarnation is not an accepted theory for Western people. His response was very profound, and one I'll always remember. He said, "But if you don't put it in, you don't give them a chance."

What Lama Zopa wanted to avoid was prejudging who was going to accept something wholly, who was going to accept something but not be affected by it (an intermediate stage of understanding), and who was going to reject it entirely. He at least wanted to give readers a chance to think about it. That's how I feel about reincarnation, too, and why it was important for me to introduce this seminal topic in this book.

What If It Isn't in the Room?

This dialogue between Eastern and Western modes of thinking is present in every area of spiritual and intellectual discourse. I am reminded about how His Holiness the Dalai Lama phrased one critique about psychotherapy: "What if what we're talking about isn't in the room?"

What he was referring to are the past karmic imprints that are coming to fruition and causing whatever manner of trouble is experienced in this life, while both the psychologist and the client are resolute in only discussing the origin and evolution of problems in this present lifetime.

From the Buddhist perspective, how else would you explain the infinite multitude of differences between people that are present from birth? Perhaps people will say that everything is materialistic, and any difference must be based in the baby's DNA. But the mind is formless, not material, not even existent on an atomic or molecular level. How then are the causes of mental disorders and mental experience explained by the psychologist? These are formless experiences, yes, that cannot, scientifically or logically, arise from a cause that is discordant with the effect. Otherwise, acorns could produce Teslas. In fact, everything would be random. An effect needs to have a similar nature as its cause. Mental experiences are formless and thus produce formless results, whereas DNA is form and produces results in form. Then the question can arise: "How is the genetic material created, and by whom? What is the substantial cause?" Buddhists respond that the previous life's imprints are carried on the consciousness as it departs from the previous body at death and enters the new embryo at conception.

This question, "What if it isn't in the room?" is especially important when a therapist is a convinced Buddhist. If you are a convinced Buddhist, then you cannot completely ignore or disregard the law of cause and effect—that is, karma and its imprints. Rather, when we study cause and effect and mental imprints, more and more one comes to see that afflictive emotions, mental disorders, and, in fact, all mental and emotional experiences arise from past imprints. If we are to incorporate the principles of karma, not only might these afflictions be rooted in the past before this life, it is believed that these imprints are in fact primarily rooted in the past before this life. This is not to say that these habits of manifesting imprints are not reinforced through events and circumstances in this life. They are. But the actual imprint, the karmic seed, was most likely generated during one's most recent past life, the life before that, or even many lives ago. When the seed "sprouts," it is watered by habits that have continued from the past, as well as reinforcement from conditions in this life. Experiences in early childhood continue to reinforce and recreate similar causes or imprints later in life, like how early experience with an abusive parent often carries significant impacts for a child well into adulthood.

The whole thrust of Buddhist mental wellness is rooted in the intention of completely ridding the mind of all afflictive emotions and delusions. This cannot be done without vanquishing from the mind the seeds of mental disorders. In therapy, and, really, in all relief from suffering or dissatisfactoriness or problemness that we seek, we are trying to calm the effects of the mental imprints. But, as I often say, this is like trying to eat burned popcorn. You cannot put the popcorn back into the kernel and hope to cook it again; you can only hope to season it so it is not so distasteful. When in my practice I've had a client in my office crying because, say, their partner has cheated on them, I have the obvious concern to help the client out of their distress. But, that may not solve the problem long term, at least from the Buddhist perspective. While the client is experiencing the distress of the betrayal, the previous imprints are ripening and, in fact, being exhausted. They have been "popped," as in our popcorn analogy, and we cannot undo that—we cannot unpop the corn.

There are a couple of deep problems that a Buddhist psychologist would present here: How many more kernels are there remaining to be popped? How do this client's reactions—anger, hurt, depression, revenge—eliminate future challenges or, alternately, create a whole new set of imprints that will ripen in a similar way in the future? This is why the suffering we are involved in is called "the cycle of samsara." It just never ends, unless one intervenes with wisdom rather than just reactiveness. This is not at all meant to blame the victim, nor forgive or "absolve" the transgressor for their indiscretions. Rather, this is the route to freedom for the woman in question; his karma will follow them as surely as it does for all of us.

The context of Buddhist psychology allows us to become even more skilled in understanding the nature of the mind and consciousness. With a little reflection and meditation, one can see that the mind is not something fixed or static. It is constantly moving. The present mental moment has arisen from the previous moment, resides for an instant—an imperceptible instant, except for the advanced meditator—and then dissolves, allowing the next mental moment to arise. When one watches this process, one can retrace where each moment has arisen. One goes back five minutes, then one day, then one week, then regresses all the way back to childhood and infancy to look for the first moment of one's experience. But each moment is a series of arising and falling; this is a characteristic of cause and effect. When one gets back to the moment of conception, when the present consciousness enters the embryo, one still cannot find some sort of beginning. Any beginning must have had a cause, since moments exist in a progression, a series, an arising. So that first moment of consciousness in this life must also have a catalyst, a previous thought or mental experience. If not, then where did that first moment come from? And since it produces an effect, it too must also be caused by something; if it had no cause, it would have no effect. It would be static, permanent, and something that is "unproduced." An unproduced entity cannot, ever, produce something. I realize this must sound very heady, but eventually we must be our own psychologist, our own philosopher, and seek these profound ideas through personal experience. That way you can validate or dismiss them.

Now, the good news is that we do not need to just wait until we experience the ripening of past imprints in order to be free of them. Since these imprints are not an inseparable part of our being, of our true nature, they can be eliminated through a plethora of techniques when accompanied by a wise perspective. In therapy or in one's personal experience, the sensation that "something deeper might be afoot" is the pesky way that problems indicate for us that they will be difficult to change. That can be true even with a deeper approach, like Buddhist practice, which, we could say, is Buddhist therapy. The process of overcoming these problems is slow, but I believe the result is significantly better. Again, this is not for everyone, and the ability to engage in this deeply transformative work depends on where someone is in their development, state of mind, or life circumstances. This is not say there is not something useful for everyone in this approach, but this kind of determination demands wisdom of the teacher or therapist. A buddha—someone who has attained the final state of omniscience—can deliver that kind of determination as someone who has this omniscient wisdom and knows exactly the right intervention for each person's unique circumstance. Only a buddha, an enlightened consciousness, really knows the exact thing to do all the way to one's awakening. This is not to say that other people, and other practitioners with experience, also cannot be helpful. But in the context of showing us the path to liberation, we are being picky.

There is a story of the Buddha's wisdom that I have always appreciated, in which he is with one of his disciples, a very simple monk in the monastery who could not remember in the evening what he had learned in the morning. The Buddha told him, "When you sweep, you are cleansing your mind. Repeat to yourself, 'I am cleaning the dust and grime in my mind. My mind is perfectly cleansed.'" Through this simple practice the monk attained liberation. Liberation occurs when the mind is thoroughly cleaned of all mental afflictions and the mind's true nature of clarity with wisdom is attained. So the advice the Buddha gave to this monk acted as a powerful metaphor.

Stories like this from the Buddha's lifetime are relevant to the therapeutic context where a person is asking for the therapist's help to be free of pain and suffering. As one of my mentors once told me, "Karuna, you cannot coach someone who doesn't ask to be coached." That's why we need to have the wisdom to understand what is best for a person and not just rely on what we think is best for them. There is a saying among Buddhists, "When you meet a beggar on the road, don't preach philosophy but give him some food."

One Life to Enlightenment or Many?

Ridding our mind and consciousness of negative karmic imprints can seem like an exhausting, even impossible, process. To that I would say: you have no idea! In popular Buddhist literature it is explained that Shakyamuni Buddha, the historical buddha who demonstrated enlightenment and brought the present teachings into the world, took three countless, great eons to traverse the path that culminated in his final attainment of enlightenment under the Bodhi Tree in India about 2,600 years ago. An eon is one of the amusing concepts that is very difficult to comprehend, but Buddhism, being rather courageous in exploring difficult concepts, has some robust explanations of what exactly an eon is. It is beyond the scope of this book to detail the difference between a small, medium, great, and "countless" eon or describe how intermediate eons make up full eons and so on. For the sake of this conversation, let's just say that one eon is the length of time to cover the following four phases of time: the time it takes for a sun, or star, to evolve to its full potential, the time it sustains that full potential before starting to fade, the fading period, and then the "dark" period that occurs after it has disappeared and before another sun arises in its place.

In other words, it is billions and billions of years. During that time, a living being continues to go in and out of countless incarnations. A "countless great eon" is inconceivably longer than the eon presented above. Since we have existed since beginningless time, we have had countless rebirths and have created countless karmic seeds. When those seeds ripen, we create new ones as well, so it just goes on forever . . . unless one intervenes and cuts this cycle. That is what liberation is, and enlightenment is the final liberation. Everything after that is pure happiness. Additionally, once a person merely enters the path, in Shakyamuni Buddha's case at the very beginning of the first eon, one's life forever is transformed, and one progresses from happiness to greater happiness until finally reaching enlightenment. So there is no simple dichotomy of us "lowly" people here and "those enlightened ones" out there. There are also "awakening beings," which is the label for people who are on the path that will result in liberation or enlightenment. An awakening being, having entered the path, is the meaning of a spiritual practitioner in the Buddhist context.

So here we have the concept of a "path." For the Buddha, that path took three countless great eons to traverse, wherein he had millions of rebirths in various forms. But from the very beginning of the path, he was no longer an "ordinary being." That will happen to us, too. Maybe it's already started—who knows where we are on that continuum. Now, the beauty of this path is that there are certain practices where the whole process can be truncated to a much shorter time frame. It is explained in the texts that a person can attain enlightenment in sixteen lifetimes, seven lifetimes, three lifetimes, and even one single lifetime. The time frame depends on the type of technique the practitioner is engaged in as well as the person's capacity, or capability, and motivation. In the Tibetan tradition, there are a number of renown sages who attained enlightenment, it is said, in a single lifetime. The most famous of these is the beloved saint Milarepa.

I was once in attendance at a three-day teaching by His Holiness the Dalai Lama in Los Angeles. The topic of the series of talks was developing the altruistic aspiration to attain enlightenment for the benefit of all living beings. In the Buddhist teachings, this is referred to as *bodhichitta* in Sanskrit, which literally translates as the "awakening mind." Bodhichitta is the single most essential teaching, along with the teachings on reality, for the Great Vehicle (Mahayana) Buddhist. In the Great Vehicle, it is commonly said that wisdom (the understanding of reality) without this great compassion (bodhichitta) is like a bird trying to fly with one wing. It is this sense of responsibility to the welfare of others that drives the practitioner to attain enlightenment. This enlightenment is not solely for the benefit of oneself, then, but it is for the benefit of all living beings. For only by extracting oneself from the prison of the world can one truly help others. Once someone develops this attitude, they are referred to as a *bodhisattva*, meaning "awakening being."

After teaching for three days on this extraordinary attitude, His Holiness invited questions from the audience. One of the questions drew a strong response from

His Holiness. The person asked, "What is the quickest way to achieve enlightenment?"

At the time, I thought this was a great question. I felt that this questioner really had a strong concern for the welfare of others and wanted to quickly traverse the path so that he could begin to really have a positive effect on the world. His Holiness saw it differently.

To my surprise, the Dalai Lama began by reprimanding the questioner. In fact, he admonished all of us Westerners for always wanting the quickest result. He commented that our Western materialism was training us to expect everything to be achieved with ease and swiftly. While there are Buddhist practices that can actually facilitate the attainment of enlightenment in several lifetimes, even one lifetime, the example he quoted was that of Shakyamuni Buddha, whose journey to enlightenment was above described as taking the same length of time as it does for a sun to come into existence, abide, and disintegrate, plus the "dark" time until another one begins to form. Our present sun, for reference, is believed to have been formed 4.5 billion years ago, and scientists say it is still expanding.

So it took this long for Shakyamuni to attain full awakening, but it should be noted that after the first great eon that passed once he entered into the practice, he did achieve direct insight into reality, and then for the next two eons he cultivated that insight until he achieved full enlightenment. Perhaps by the notion of "instant enlightenment," people mean this direct insight into reality. But even then, one is still far away from full awakening and the complete freedom it brings. Also, it is important to note that one can have insight into reality that is not a direct insight, as it is still mixed with conceptual thought, before getting very far down the path. Because the person has likely not developed single-pointed concentration through meditation, their insight will wane and just be a distant memory after a short period of time. But, at the same time, that insight is more easily retrievable than having never generated it.

If There Are Future Lives, Was There a First One?

I have found that one of the consistent sticking points for Western-educated people interested in Buddhism is the notion of origins of the universe and living beings. So let me put forth a couple of assumptions that Buddhist thought does not agree with. The first is that there was a beginning to this mess, a kind of big bang to our personal existence along with the existence of the physical universe. The second is that there is a supreme being or some primal essence that is the source of everything. Buddhism rejects these two constructs right off the bat.

While Buddhist cosmology does present six different realms of existence—among them the human realm, animal realm, spirit realm, and hell realm—none of these realms are inhabited by a supreme, omnipotent being. There are multiple realms with celestial beings, but they are not omnipotent, eternal, omniscient, or liberated. They too eventually die and become humans, animals, hell beings, and so forth. Why? Because our consciousness has no beginning and no end. It continues to cycle and cycle and cycle. However, while consciousness has no end, the ignorance that envelops the consciousness can end. That's what the path will accomplish, and that end state is the full awakening called buddhahood. The state of buddhahood is not the same as being a supreme being; while buddhas are omniscient, they are not omnipotent or all-powerful, like you would imagine a creator god would be. If that being were all-powerful, then they would have eliminated all suffering by now.

It is extremely difficult for those of us in the West to wrap our heads around the idea that our mind has no beginning, that there was not some divine spark or cardinal sin that started all of this off. Neither are we suffering as punishment for having eaten of the tree of knowledge, and so on. One's life is not some divine trick that all started with ignorance, because there is no start to begin with. It just is.

The mind is a stream of consciousness, a stream of endless and beginningless experience. With a modicum of meditation experience, and by choosing the mind as one's object of meditation, investigation, and study, one can see the continual movement of the mind as it goes from one thought to the other, one mental image to the other, one sensation experience to the other. The mind never stops cognizing or experiencing, even if we are not aware of these experiences. The advanced meditator is aware of these experiences, and as they progress they are able to see the even subtler mental experiences that are completely unknown to us. All the information of the world—inner and outer—comes within their grasp. I often say that clairvoyance is no big deal. The information is there; we just don't access it. I think of it like taking a smartphone into a nontechnological culture, say a remote indigenous tribe in the Amazon. If you were to take out your smartphone and predict that it will rain tomorrow or there will be an eclipse, you would be seen as a prophet to the indigenous people, when we all know that you just had access to information that is already there.

Rather than focusing on these questions about origin, it is far more valuable to perceive the links between what you experience now and your past, and then to make the association with the future that is going to come. You can create the world you want to live in, both for yourself and for countless other beings. The problem with the modern-day approaches of life-coaching or self-realization is these movements think that you can quickly create the world you want to live in, the future you wish to create, just by wishing it or visualizing it and applying positive affirmations. Examples abound of what we might call a "manifestation" theology: If you want it, will it. That's unfortunately misleading. Or we can say, they're kind of right, but they've got their timing all wrong.

Let's take manifesting wealth or abundance as an example. Many people have taken this approach to heart, and they've actually done it—abundance manifested for them. What they don't tell you is that abundance didn't manifest for a lot of other people . . . and no one knows why. They might say you didn't commit to it or didn't try hard enough. Those people who generated abundance, they thought about, projected, and visualized abundance and then got the result, so there must be something wrong with you. What they don't understand is that there have to first be the imprints, the karma, in order to get the result. The results did not manifest because there was something unseen that was missing.

For a Buddhist, the reason why something is not manifesting—why we're not generating millions of dollars or achieving any of our other wildest dreams—is because we have imprints that are blocking it, lack the imprints to bring those results, or both. Continuing with this example, in theory you could purify those obstructive imprints and also create the positive imprints of abundance if you don't have them. In theory, then, you could manifest abundance for this life and no one would be wanting for anything. But to know this, you would first want to know how deep the negative imprints lay that were preventing abundance. There could be very few of them, and those might reside very shallowly in your consciousness—light imprints that can purify quickly. On the other hand, you could be dealing with lifetimes of greed, the effects of which you are now tasked with eradicating if you want to achieve your goal. To purify those imprints would be a very intense and hard process that took a very long time.

Regardless of the level and intensity of the imprint, however, you really only need one thing to create a positive imprint. In order to manifest things, you have to have intentions, and with Buddhism we whittle it down to just this one intention: the intention of the awakening mind, bodhichitta. You can say to yourself, "I'm doing this to achieve the fully compassionate, awakened state of being for the benefit of others in particular, as well as myself."

When this is your intention, then you really know what's helpful to people and how you can best help. It doesn't matter whether you're working in a hospital or in your business. It doesn't matter whether the object of your compassion is your clientele, your readers, or your patients. If you are really seeking to help people by offering a service, then you will do the action and rejoice. You will feel satisfied in what you've done—or with your attempt, because it's okay if it's just an attempt. We don't have control over the outcome, but we can control our intention. There are all sorts of other factors at play; whether you are successful or not is not really up to you. It has to do with karmic imprints, yours as well as theirs. Whether you can help someone else is never a guarantee.

Rebirth in a Pure Land

Let's look at a particularly lofty goal: You think you want to be reborn in the pure land or heaven in your next life. You're convinced, first, that you will have a next life. And from that, you make the intention of being reborn in that pure realm, where you can continue your spiritual practice in a more powerful, focused, and intense way. You think your progress will go quicker for you there. And so the object of your practice is to have the direct result of being born in the pure lands. There are some actions, some practices, and some behaviors that have the direct result of generating wealth in the future. A practice of charity and generosity, for example, results in wealth in the future. If you want to live in a pure land, as in this example, then you have to perform other kinds of virtuous actions. Maybe after one of those virtuous activities, your morning meditation practice or the completion of a longer retreat, you feel very satisfied and actually quite happy because you know that because of what you did, you will experience your desired result.

The funny thing about us is that right now—and this is really important to reflect on—in this very moment, we are living the future rebirth of our previous life. There was a time and a place in the past when you created the causes to be where you are now. Maybe you were a sheepherder or a monk or a nun, or maybe you were a businessperson or a family person, and you had the concept that what you do in this life will result in a better future life or afterlife. That's a very core belief for many people, not just Buddhists. In one form or another, it applies to all of the world's religions.

Back in that previous life, you would never imagine this incredible future life that you have now; it's very likely your life then wasn't as good as it is now. Just think how fortunate you are to have the time and resources to read this book right now! You achieved it; pat yourself on the back. You did this, no one else. You created the cause to be reborn where you now live. You could be in countless other places right now.

So we're here because of the imprints we created. If you like your life, then keep doing what you're doing. If you don't like it, do other things more. Someday you'll be in your future life, just like you're in this one right now after your previous life. What do you want that future life to look like? Either way, moving on to your next life is guaranteed, whether you're a believer in reincarnation or not. Not believing in something doesn't make it not real. So when I say "guaranteed," it is from the conviction, through a lot of analysis and reflection, that reincarnation is a fact. What's not guaranteed is that everything you want will manifest in this life. But it will manifest at some point, given that you've created the causes, and then you'll wonder, "How did I create this? How did I get so lucky?"

Hope for the Future

The actual condition in which we live, as we have been discussing throughout this book, is pervasive suffering—or what we can also call dissatisfactoriness or problemness. This is because we are born with mental imprints that continue to arise and create our reality. In addition, we inherit various afflictions, chief among which are ignorance, attachment, and aversion. Due to our inherent lack of control—the control that comes from developing the wisdom that sees the reality of how things really exist—we react to the imprints that arise and the afflictive or disturbing emotions that follow them like a shadow. We are born set up for difficulty. It's in the package.

You may have experienced this in a meditation: how sometimes it feels like you have zero control over which mental imprints are going to arise. In an instant, we could be thrown into a mental hell. Or there can be a gradual cascade of problems that seems to have no solutions, no matter how many doctors and specialists we consult, how many business advisors we seek counsel from, no matter how many friends or lovers we gather, no matter how abundant our resources are or how many items we collect. We just have no control over whether things will work in our favor, will endure for any length of time, or whether a given situation will turn to crap. We are quite literally feathers in the wind, blown every which way. And of course, the same is true with the unfolding of good things. It just seems like the good things are harder to achieve and maintain.

Well, here's the good news: Because the mind is in the nature of change and because the afflictions are not an inherent part of the mind itself, we can become completely free of negative mental imprints, afflictions, and their accompanying mental disorders. There is a state of freedom and liberation that can be achieved where it is finally possible to say bye-bye to the beginningless problems we have faced up to now. And while this state of being is not instantly achieved, we can improve year by year merely by entering into the process of achieving awakening. To become happier year by year, even month by month, and eventually day by day: that alone is a miracle worth working toward.

7
Conclusion

There is a common instruction given by Buddhist teachers to students attending their classes. We are told not to be like a jug that is upside-down, has a hole in it, or is dirty. The analogy here is that an upside-down jug is completely closed off to listening to new ideas. The jug with a hole in it is the person who listens but retains none of the information; they may be too distracted to have any of the ideas sink in. The third analogy, the dirty jug, is the person so filled up with their own ideas and concepts that they criticize the ideas they are hearing or change them to fit their preconceived theories. To really listen is not only a dying art, it seems, but extremely difficult for us modern, hyperactive people.

By reflecting on the material in this book, we might, at first, just be planting a little bit of doubt about how what we thought was the case is not the case after all. There are myths we live by, but there are other truths, laws, and understandings we can access instead. If we've been working with these ideas for a while, then this material can deepen our relationship with the way we see our life, our potential, and the nature of our struggles and achievements. We need to remember that all of this exploration and thinking is to create a better life for ourselves and others. If our study and curiosity just lead to more unhappiness after a prolonged period of trying to apply the ideas, then maybe it is better to move on to another approach.

When Lama Thubten Yeshe knew he was ill and would die in a few months, he said, "I'm satisfied with my life. I did my best." We can speculate on how he arrived at this place of peace and contentment, but I think it starts with not taking life for granted. This life is an extraordinarily precious gift. We take for granted our health, our security, our friendships, our environment, and a hundred other things. Of course, people will argue that they are unfortunate because they don't have a partner, or they lost their job, or they live in a cramped apartment. And, yes, some people do have tough, even seemingly impossible conditions. But just think how animals, and many people as well, cannot access the ideas in this book that offer a pathway to real happiness—the real potential that each being has. We need to know what that potential is. And that is why *Six Myths We Live By* is, in the end, upbeat and hopeful. Each of us has the potential to have a more balanced mind, which is a preliminary goal on the way to the ultimate end goal: to be fully free.

Part 2

The Practices

8
Introduction to Meditation

One of the pitfalls facing us modern people is that we are information junkies. We mistake the acquiring of information with actually knowing something. Years ago, one of my younger son's friends was a voracious researcher and reader. He would search the internet for the answers to all his questions in life. When faced with the prospect of trying out for his high school baseball team, having never played in a game or really even tossed a baseball around, he dove into a digital rabbit hole on the proper mechanics of hitting a baseball. When the time came for him to try out for the team, he obviously was unable to perform. This may seem like a pretty ordinary example of the difference between knowledge and wisdom, but understanding that difference becomes especially relevant when engaging in a spiritual path of inner development as it is articulated by the Buddhist masters.

Lama Yeshe used to provoke us by saying that if knowledge were enough, then every college professor teaching Buddhism and other comparative religions would be enlightened! He would point out that these same professors were often a mess when it came to living a wholesome and balanced life. The same can be said for psychologists and marriage counselors. It always struck me as odd that a popular marriage counselor could go through a messy divorce. On the other hand, that experience might give them more credibility. In fact, that is where we come to the Buddhist philosopher as guide.

It is strongly argued in Buddhism, at least in the Buddhism I have been engaged with, that one has to "walk the talk" if one is to be regarded as an authority. This absolutely does not mean that in order to teach and guide others one needs to be enlightened. That's neither practical nor realistic. But one must accept that to be a spiritual guide, one needs to be a practitioner of the teachings and philosophy one is espousing. One has to be, as much as possible for their experience level, authentic. A guide has to be at least a little bit more advanced in knowledge and experience than those they are guiding. The students could be more advanced than their teachers, and that would not be an issue if there were a clear understanding and appreciation of where the teachers' limitations were and if they were transparent about what they were still striving to attain. Complete honesty. Complete humility.

It is in that spirit, then, that I offer six different meditations here, one for each of the myths we have been introduced to over the course of this book. The subject of meditation is pretty misunderstood in modern culture vis-à-vis its traditional roots in Buddhism. I actually prefer the term *mind training* over *meditation*. The word for meditation in the Tibetan language, as derived from its Sanskrit definition, actually means "to become familiar" or "to familiarize." But if I asked a hundred people who are unfamiliar with Buddhist thought what the definition of *meditation* is, I doubt anyone would say "to familiarize."

To "become familiar" has a deep connotation here. One becomes familiar with an object through experiencing that object. For example, we listen to and study teachings about impermanence. We hear about gross impermanence and subtle impermanence. We contemplate this and the fact that there is both internal impermanence (related to the mind and mental factors) and external impermanence (related to the outer world of rocks, people, buildings, and so on). But when we get to the stage of meditating on impermanence, that is when we actually engage with impermanence. We see it before our mind's eye and even the physical eye. As Lama Yeshe used to say, "We taste the cheesecake." We're no longer looking at the cheesecake, thinking about the cheesecake, learning how to make the cheesecake. We are finally having the full experience of the sweetness, texture, and sensations that come from actually eating a piece.

The point is that experience is everything in Buddhism and Buddhist practice. I've found there is a general sense of respect for any scholar of Buddhist thought, but Buddhists don't typically feel any overall devotion to that person as a guide. Being learned is not such a big deal in traditional Buddhist circles—that is, if it is divorced from experience and the actual behaviors and attitudes that would match the person's academic or intellectual understanding.

In the early days after I arrived in Nepal, I went to visit my very first Tibetan lama. He was a layperson with a family, but was well known as an experienced meditator and teacher. I was only twenty-one years old, and at that time was transitioning out of Hinduism because my guru had been a little bit controversial; in my thinking, I couldn't harmonize his behavior with his teachings. That happens. But I had nonetheless developed an affection for the practice of guru devotion, which is a central part of Hinduism. So I asked Rinpoche how one can find a reliable guru.

Rinpoche said to me something I'd never heard before nor knew I even had permission to think about. He replied, "When you meet a teacher, you should examine him over a period of time. You should examine him, examine him, and examine him some more. And, when you find he's at fault, nail him to the wall like a fly!"

I was taken aback, to say the least. But I was also relieved. Of course, he did not mean this literally, since Buddhists do not kill and he would never mean literally to "nail a fly to the wall." But this honesty, rawness, and provocation were just what I needed to hear, and I have never forgotten it. It is a fundamentally beautiful thing that Buddhism encourages in the student—critical thinking. This allows us to critically examine any teacher as to what qualifies they possess, or do not possess, that can help guide us in assessing to what level they can help us. It may be they can assist us in our meditation practice or our understanding of Buddhist concepts, but not necessarily guide us all the way to enlightenment. For a teacher to possess the qualities to guide a student on the full path to awakening is rare, and not to be taken as a given just because the teacher wears robes, is an articulate speaker, or has charisma we find alluring.

So the key to meditation is experience. It is only through experience that we can change significantly. The way one experiences the topic of a teaching, like impermanence, is to first learn to calm the mind significantly and develop a sense of awareness and mental sharpness, as opposed to just spacing out or feeling blissful. We then use that heightened awareness and focus to integrate the mind with the topic. When the tool of meditation is honed, after a lot of discipline and time, then whatever you set the mind on can generate a realization of that topic. With impermanence, for example, the mind directly interacts and "fuses" with impermanence. When you look at the external world, everything becomes soft, fluid, and moving . . . just like it truly is. Even the mind's impermanence is seen as clearly as a stone in one's hand.

As I just mentioned, a prerequisite for developing the meditative mind is to learn to settle the mind. The breath is a perfect object of focus for this because it is completely neutral, natural, and easily accessible. We don't want to romanticize the breath—it just is. But many of us are into pleasure and excitement, and before long we will become bored with such a simple bodily function, so we begin to fantasize and elaborate the breath. And this is the exact beauty of using the breath as an object of focus. While using the breath as our object, all of the mind's foibles will helpfully reveal themselves. We will fall prey to an expectation about what we are achieving, a desire for more depth and insight, making plans for all the realizations we're going to attempt to achieve—all of these are typical distractions. The meditation instructions offered next are designed to help you stay with the breath so that you can then fuse with each individual topic to come, and thus realize for yourself how these myths are playing out in your everyday life.

Baseline Instructions for Meditation

Sit comfortably. You can even lie down if you don't feel you will doze off. Ideally, you can sit cross-legged on the floor with your bottom slightly raised by a comfortable pillow or cushion. Let your back be straight like an arrow but soft and relaxed. The shoulders, too, should be relaxed. Your chin is just slightly bent downward, maybe not more than an inch. The eyes are gently closed or slightly opened. Your hands go on your lap, with the right hand resting on the left one, the arms just slightly and comfortably away from your sides. Generally, the feet rest on the thighs in what is known as the lotus position, but this can be too stressful for many of us. You can have one foot on a thigh and the other underneath you on the floor, or both feet on the floor. You can also sit in a chair if that is more comfortable and less of a distraction. If you sit in a chair, just make sure your back is straight—not ramrod straight, but straight and easy—and best if your feet are flat on the floor. You will know you have chosen a correct posture because it simply keeps you alert and—this is the big point—it allows you to forget about the body as it is now in its place for the job at hand.

Next, do a quick body scan starting at your crown,

checking if there is any tension in your face, jaw, neck, shoulders, arms, chest, abdomen, hips, thighs, calves, or feet. If you sense some tension, just feel your breath move through those areas. You can even sense how the tension gently flows down through your feet and absorbs into the ground, like when you water a plant.

Now find your breath. It may be at the tip of the nostrils or within the rising and falling of your abdomen. Do not manipulate it. Do not control it. Do not do anything with it. You're just an observer. It's like watching street traffic from a high building—if it's congested or light, you can't do anything. Just watch.

Now your job starts. I recommend beginning with five-minute sessions and slowly working your way up to twenty-four minutes. In the traditional texts for developing single-pointed concentration, it is suggested to do twenty-four-minute sessions throughout the day and into the night. Sessions that are short like this are believed to be more effective. As Lama Yeshe used to say, "We should end our meditation session before we want to. That way we'll want to come back. Otherwise, our meditation cushion will begin to look like a bed of nails!" Lama would add that just like everyone likes to climb into their comfortable bed, the meditation area should inspire the same feeling. You should feel attracted to it. Certain practices demand more austerity, but generally we look for the "middle way."

To assist with your focus on the breath, mentally count each exhalation: "One" . . . then "Two" on the next exhalation . . . up to twenty-one. Then, repeat the same process, counting backward from twenty-one to one. One round like this in the beginning is good enough.

Eventually you can expand it to three rounds. Later on, you can just set a timer. Remember to set the timer to just short of when you want to finish, before you become fatigued.

Once your mind has settled using this method, you can take up the individual meditations that follow for each of the myths. But before we get to that, let me just say that you will find yourself distracted. Be aware of these distractions as they enter the mind. The purpose of this practice is not to try to stop distractions, other than keeping your focus on the breath. Being aware of distractions is actually a big part of the practice. You don't necessarily try to stop them because there is more wisdom in noticing them as they try to steal your attention. This mindfulness of distractions is a powerful tool in reshaping your life as you go through your day, your week, your year, your life. It is what allows us to develop mental control.

Remember that when you are meditating, you don't need to build a twenty-foot brick wall around your mind whose job is to keep all distractions at bay. Trying to avoid distractions will only create tension, frustration, and fatigue. It will actually aid the distractions in getting a hold of you. The mind then becomes even more agitated or dull. Your job is to have attentive relaxation and to notice the distractions as they come into the mind. At this level of practice, you are not doing anything with the distractions, but this not-doing is actually doing quite a bit. Why? Because it is human nature to run toward or away from just about everything that comes into the mind. After a few seconds of meditation, you're off fantasizing about what you're going to eat for breakfast, who you're going to meet later today, the email you are going to write to the person who was rude to you, the great spiritual attainments you're going to achieve through your meditation . . . and on and on and on. At this stage, you are being a successful meditator if you are noticing the distraction and simply not clinging or sticking to whatever is arising in the mind. Let the distraction arise, abide for a moment, and then fade into the space of your mind. There's nothing to hold on to, nothing to get excited about, nothing to fear, nothing to be sad over. It's all just dust in the wind.

Each meditation that follows has three sections: a reintroduction of the topic, so you do not need to go back to the chapter to refamiliarize yourself with exactly what is at stake with this myth; a reflection that will further prepare your mind for the meditation by exploring the opposite of each myth; and finally, a meditation, which will bring you into the experience of what lies beyond the myth in question.

9
Reality

The Topic

The foundation of the Buddhist psychological approach to freedom and happiness is the unveiling of the correct view of reality. All problems that we have been trapped in, from beginningless time to now, have their cause in the fact that we do not see reality. As Geshe Gelek said, "We see what isn't there and we don't see what is there." So if we are constantly interacting with, reacting to, pursuing, clinging to, or desiring something that is not there—in the way it is perceived, anyhow—how can this ever lead to complete and sustaining contentment? And lack of contentment means a lack of freedom; it means being constantly under the control of events, of others, and of conditions.

Simply put, "reality" means something appears the way it actually exists. A mirage off in the distance appears as water, yet the mirage does not exist as it appears; it is not reality. Your mind is tricked. And that is exactly what happens to us every second of the day and night.

Of course, the mug in front of you does exist . . . just

not the way it appears. We have never seen anything as it actually exists. There are many aspects to this "lack of seeing reality." In fact, there are four Buddhist philosophical schools that developed in India, and each presents increasingly subtle explanations of how we misperceive things and the actual correct view of how things exist, both in terms of external objects and the self.

I will not go into those subtle explanations here, but I will point out that there are three ways in which most objects, as well as the self, appear to exist yet are false. First, things appear to exist "over there" as an independent, standalone, complete entity. Second, things appear to have no parts, as if the thing is a monolithic, solid, singular entity. Third, things appear as if they are unchanging, permanent, and static. These three qualities also apply to our sense of self and the way we perceive our identity, our "I" and "me."

Everything we experience in life—every sense perception of sights, sounds, and so on; every thought, feeling, and opinion—is viewed wrongly. When we view wrongly, that also means we respond wrongly to this erroneous feedback that we get from our perceptions. We see all these experiences as either independent, partless, and permanent or at least one of these all the time. And if that is not the way they exist—and not the way "I" exist—then what are the consequences of viewing life in this way? From the Buddhist view, the consequence is a life that is absent of freedom, everlasting joy, and ultimate ease. And the absence of these qualities is the absence of true happiness, our birthright.

Reflection

As with all of these exercises, begin by spending a few minutes settling the mind. Just watch the inhalation and exhalation of the breath through the nostrils. If the mind is particularly unsettled, then you can watch the breath by observing the stomach area going in and out. Just do this twenty-one times, with each exhalation counting as one; stay focused in order to not lose count. Some people demand of themselves that they start over again if they lose count. But whatever works for you to experience the brightening of the mind that comes from increased clarity will do just fine.

Now, gently reflect on how you go from one experience to the other looking for pleasure or satisfaction and how this seems an endless process. Next, reflect on how you must be tricked by your perception of things as permanent, partless, and independent so that you are continually recruited into a view that must be mistaken. We are continually invited to pursue this or that object the way it appears to us, with the promise of satisfaction once we get it. But we never arrive at that state.

Reflect on how habituated you have become to these wrong perceptions. If these things *did* exist the way they appeared, and you attained them, then you would be content. And because that object would be permanent, it could never fade from your experience. It would be lasting and eternal. This is not the case.

We see ice cream as something permanent and thus satisfying. We don't see the ice cream as a limited pleasure provider because of our wrong view of it. See each of your desired objects as a similar misperception. And the same misperception happens with objects we don't like and want to get away from or avoid.

Meditation

Now let's bring the focus a little deeper. Focus on the inhalation/exhalation at the nostrils, or stomach if that's more comfortable. This time count to ten and then count backward to one. If you can do this for three rounds, that is best.

As the mind now is settled and focused, turn your attention to a thought or feeling. Don't lose your attention. Don't wander. Look solidly at the thought that has arisen and become "familiar" with it as appearing unchanging and existing solidly, independently, "over there." Study it and experience its appearance as something that exists inherently, as it appears. Don't overanalyze it or psychoanalyze yourself, but go deeper into the experience of it appearing solid, permanent, and independent. Stay with it until you experience the conviction that if it were permanent, it would not arise, abide, and fade away. Notice how it does do this, and yet the mind is tricked into seeing it in the opposite way. You want to see this and not just think about it. But do it very gently, like admiring a painting in a museum.

Either now in this session or in another session, change the object of engagement to your sense of self, the "I."

Say to yourself something like, "I'm meditating here," or "I'm sitting here," or just "I'm here." Very strongly gaze at the "you," the experiencer.

See now how the self or "I" appears to you as solid,

permanent, and independent of anything. The purpose here is not to see the self as existing in its true sense, but to first be aware of how this wrong view appears to the mind. To see the correct view, one must see the wrong view and become "educated" in it.

Next, observe the correct view of the self. With just a slight analysis in order to enhance the experiential view, notice that the object of your perception—not the self, at this point, but a thought or an object of sight, smell, sound, taste, or sensation—while appearing as solid, unchanging, and independent, is, in fact, the opposite. See how that the object is actually in the nature of constant change. See that it is dependent on so many factors, like cause and effect, an observer or experiencer, and so on. See also that while it appears as partless, it is nothing more than a countless accumulation of parts, sections, molecules, instances, and so on. After you generate this awareness of the object, sink into your experience without spacing out. Just relax in it. When it begins to fade, which it will, see if you can reengender the nonconceptual experience, and then rest in that experience once again. If you are unable to, then leave the session and feel satisfied with your efforts.

Finally, engage in the above process again, but this time use the self or "I" as the object. Apply the exact same process to this different object, which is the subject of the experience. First, find your sense of self. Look at the self as something that is constructed. It is constructed from past experiences, opinions, feelings, preferences, and so on. And if it is a construction, it is something that is dependent and not independent. Drop into this perception in a nonconceptual manner. This is your true "self." It is true because there is a person meditating, and that person is an interdependent entity and not the hallucinated self that masquerades as something independent. This true self is the one that is actually moving and not static or unchanging, one that is constructed of parts and neither monolithic nor independent. When you get a sense of the fluidity of the self, just rest in that perception. Trust it.

10
Identity

Topic

In many ways we can say the myth of identity, like the myth of reality, is a core myth that is at the root of every myth. It is the myth that is the primary antithesis to the state of freedom, liberation. When the myth of identity is eliminated, one's true nature then begins to reveal itself. But when the myth of identity is active, as it has been for countless lifetimes, then one's own pure, luminous mind—one's real identity—lies dormant and obscured.

Because we believe in the myth of identity, all sorts of other problems, instability, and mental and emotional dis-eases arise. Imagine, for example, that someone criticizes you harshly, unfairly even. The words and that person are outside of you until you perceive them with your ears and eyes. At that point, it's all you. You feel hurt, angry, and defensive. But *who* feels hurt, angry, and defensive? The "I" does! That "I" is the one we are talking about. If that "I" were not there, then there would be no disturbance in one's mind. So the whole event, both the inner and outer conditions, are dependent upon each other. And remember, if something is dependent, it cannot also be independent. Both the outer conditions, the harsh words, and the inner conditions, the experience of the "I," appear independent but are clearly dependent. The "I" is a dependent occurrence. Now if that "I" were detached from the event to a certain degree, then the problem would be much less, right? On the Buddhist path of awakening, the practitioner reconfigures their "I" into one that is more healthy, a person who is caring and compassionate. This is a big part of the Buddhist therapeutic approach.

The "I" seems so solid that we take its reality for granted. It is a spontaneous and reactive experience. But this "I," this "me," while appearing as a sort of an independent monarch, is really completely conditional and dependent on many, many factors. It deceives itself into thinking it is independent and self-sufficient, like a boss overseeing a large business with everyone else their staff. But in actually, the boss in this case is utterly under the control of the staff. We may go through life thinking we are in control, but, truly, the emperor has no clothes.

Reflection

As for all the reflections in this book, begin by spending a few minutes settling the mind. Just watch the inhalation and exhalation of the breath through the nostrils. If the mind is unsettled, then watch the breath at the stomach area going in and out. Just do this twenty-one times, with each exhalation counting as one; stay focused in order to not lose count.

Now, think of a difficult or stressful situation, particularly one in which you were triggered and your emotions became disturbed. It could be something someone said to you or a reoccurring argument you have with someone close to you. It could be the way your boss relates to you and tends to speak to you in a condescending way. Notice the "I" that showed up. Now reflect on how a bit later after this event, that "I" was less dominant and even faded away. Why?

Can you see how that "I" first appeared as something very concrete? Now find another identity, another moment in which your sense of identity arose strongly. This often happens when something upsetting has occurred but can also be when a strong sense of desire, longing, or hunger arises. Can you see how that "I" again appeared or presented itself, unconsciously, as who you are? Maybe the person who upset you apologized or left the room, and while you were still there being "you," you relaxed and the previous sense of "I" faded and another sense of "I," or another identity or personality, arose. Reflect on how this process seems to go on and on and on forever. Though it feels like the "I" is permanent and unchanging, intellectually, can you see how this cannot possibly be the case?

Meditation

Now bring the focus a little deeper; focus on the inhalation/exhalation at the nostrils, or stomach if that's more comfortable. Count to ten and then count backward to one. Try to do this for three rounds.

In this quiet place, bring to mind your present sense of self. You can say, "I'm sitting here." There is the sitting, the breath, then there is the experiencer. That experiencer is the "I."

Now look closely at this "I" without straining, like you're looking at a painting. Just observe it and become familiar with it as if you've never done this before. Notice how it appears to exist on its own, without parts, monolithic, unchanging and permanent, concrete. Now just hold this view without getting lost in distraction. You can feel it or see it—just experience it without conceptions or intellectualizing. Have a direct experience. Experiencing the "I" how it appears to you, even though it does not exist in that way at all, is an extremely important first step. This step alone can occupy you for months.

After you have a strong conviction, a direct insight, into the concreteness of the "I," begin to introduce another event or manifestation of that "I" from your daily life. Switch to the "I," or personality, of your work identity. Look at that identity in the exact same way you looked at your present identity when you were just sitting. Be experiential, not in your head or thoughts, as much as possible.

The next step in this process is to add analysis to your experience. This is a variation from the normal injunction against thinking or intellectualizing during meditation in favor of concentrating on experience. This is because we are in unique territory with this particular myth.

Staying focused on your experience of the concrete, permanent, unchanging, independently appearing "I," take a small part of your consciousness and examine the nature of the "I." You do not need, nor want, to lose your focus on the experience, but you will now heighten your understanding—your wisdom. This will also have the effect of strengthening your focus. This process takes practice, so in order to avoid getting frustrated, adopt the attitude of a learner or a scientist. Just be curious.

With your introspective mind, look to see exactly where this "I" is located. Again, we're talking about the experiencer here, not the experience. In other words, you're looking for the subject, not the object.

Look critically to see if you can find this "I" somewhere in your body. Is it in your legs, your chest, your head maybe? Then notice that as you look to see where it is located, there is still the experiencer somewhere else. If it is in your chest, then who is looking at your chest? If it is in your brain, who is the observer, the subject? Can you actually find it anywhere in your body where you can say, "Aha! There you are." There should be a conviction that it is nowhere to be found in the body, from the tips of the toes to the top of the head, or else you could find it and extract to out! Experience the validity of this conclusion.

If the "I" did exist within your being, then there would be only two choices for its domicile: It would either be in your body or in your mind. Which is it? If the "I" existed in the way it appears—concrete, permanent, independent, with no parts—then it must be findable in your mind, since you could not find it in your body. Focus clearly on the strong sense of "I" that is in your mind then, the one who is sitting here and investigating.

When you've reconnected with this "I," start looking for it in the mind itself. Is the "I" a feeling or sensation? If so, who is the one looking at the sensation? You may say, "I feel sad," but the sadness now is an object and not the subject. And if the "I" were the sadness itself, which part of the sadness is it? The beginning, when it arose; the abiding, which is actually changing; or the dissipation? And since this experience is moving and changing, and the "I" is permanent, how can the "I" be both permanent and impermanent? "I feel sad" changes to "I'm feeling okay now" to "I'm tired" and on and on. And this monolithic "I" watches it all, and yet thinks it is both the object, which is changing, and the subject, which seems static. This is an impossible situation.

When you cannot find this false "I," stop looking and analyzing, and focus single-pointedly on this absence of an concrete, independent, permanent "I." Rest in that spacious and empty view.

11
Permanence

Topic

The material presented in the chapter on the myth of permanence explains that just about everything is impermanent. By impermanence, we mean that nothing is static. There is both coarse impermanence, which is observable, and subtle impermanence, change at the nanosecond level that is only observable through the use of instruments or a very focused mind. The definition of impermanence is "that which is produced, a product." This means it is in a chain of cause and effect. It is dependent upon factors to come into existence. It is always in a state of change. There is almost nothing that does not change from moment to moment. Since things are produced and made up of multiple components, we say they are "compounded." And all compounded phenomena are impermanent and in the nature of change. There are just a few things that are considered uncompounded and therefore permanent. The most common is space itself. Space here means the absence of any kind of obstruction that exists between two objects.

Reflection

At this stage spend a few minutes settling the mind. Just watch the inhalation and exhalation of the breath through the nostrils. If the mind is unsettled, then you can watch the breath at the stomach area going in and out. Just do this twenty-one times, with each exhalation counting as one.

Reflect on how all physical phenomena are in a state of change. Pull up an example that is tangible for you. This can be a physical object like a car, your room, some food, music, a soft blanket, the smell of onions, and so on. You can even think of the seasons, the weeks and days that pass one into the other. At this stage you don't need to bring up an object that is too charged. In due time you can transition from using noncharged objects (there is a breeze now that wasn't there before) to charged objects (your neighbor's dog who never stops barking). You will have to judge for yourself how charged an item that you contemplate can be before it makes you lose your focus.

Whatever your object of observation, immerse yourself in it. Think about how the object is, or must be, impermanent. After a while, bring your attention to subtle change. This is a bit easier when you reflect on the fact that your thoughts, feelings, and emotions are also changing constantly. Gross phenomena, like physical things and days and seasons, are also in a state of subtle change. They are produced from previous moments, and previous moments are produced by previous seconds, nanoseconds, and so on. Think also what all this means for your attainment of lasting peace and the sustaining of your happiness. Become familiar with the fact that your happiness is built upon false premises and false perceptions. At the conclusion of this reflection you should have some sense of alignment with the idea of impermanence.

MEDITATION

Now bring the focus a little deeper by focusing on the inhalation/exhalation at the nostrils or the movement of the stomach. This time count to ten and then count backward to one. If you can do this for three rounds, that is best.

Keep your focus on the breath, but allow that focus to operate quietly in the background so that you can be aware of whatever is happening in your experience right now. It doesn't matter if it is some sensual experience, like hearing the sound of a car driving by, or a physical sensation, like your body experiencing an ache or pain, or if it is a thought or mental image that is dominant at the moment. Look directly at this experience without elaborating it with thoughts and opinions. Don't even wonder, "Is it this or is it that?" Just look. Just observe.

Staying focused on this object, observe its impermanence. See how the experience arises, abides, and disintegrates. Whatever experience comes in, whether through the senses or in the mind itself, just watch this process like you're watching a gentle stream flow by. The content in your mind, like thoughts, images, and conceptions, begin to soften and appear like clouds moving through the sky of your mind. You will have an aha moment of a direct perception of movement, impermanence, and change. When you see it, don't grasp or cling to this—it will then freeze, and you'll lose the experience. Just *be*, with awareness. Let go and flow.

12
Randomness

Topic

Why do bad things happen to good people? Or, conversely, why do good things happen to bad people? It is interesting that unless we're a scientist or looking at things religiously, we never really deeply ponder why things happen at all. And yet we ceaselessly look for causes as to why things happen. We particularly ask this question when unfortunate or painful events happen.

Simply speaking, things can happen due to one of two things: a cause or randomness. No one, strangely enough, is fully satisfied with the "random" theory. The random theory is just not tenable. If things did not happen due to a cause, and everything just randomly occurred, then the universe would be chaos. An acorn could grow a rosebush, or even a car. DNA would have no predictable effect. One could eat anything and never be satisfied because the cause, hunger, would not be alleviated by the effect, eating. One could handle plutonium and have no adverse effects, because nothing produces causes that lead to effects.

One needs to become convinced that there are only these two choices, randomness or the law of cause and effect, for explaining how things work or why they happen. We call it the "law" of cause and effect because there are rules to how one cause produces a particular effect. As you will recall from the chapter on the myth of randomness, the word *karma* means "action." There is physical action and mental action. In the practice of awakening, we are primarily concerned with mental action.

It is essential to understand that when we speak of the law of karma, or the law of cause and effect, we are speaking of a deeper understanding of this law. Typically, when we speak of cause and effect, we mean physical causes and their results. In the law of cause and effect as elucidated in Buddhist philosophy, however, there is a distinction between conditions and karma. In the conventional world, only conditions are considered within the dynamics of cause and effect. This is not what is meant in the Buddhist articulation of karmic cause and effect. Another way of saying this is that karmic cause and effect is primarily concerned with the "why"—and not the "what." When we look for the cause of an argument we may have had with someone, we talk about the what: the person arguing with us is closed-minded, having a bad day, just angry with the world, and so on. But in the law of karma, we dig deep into the why and the how, which is subtler: why the argument arose from imprints that reside on the person's consciousness.

With respect to the law of cause and effect of the mind—that is, with mental actions—we can see the mind is constantly at work. There is a continual arising and falling away of thoughts, feelings, emotions, and attitudes. This is mental karma. Given that thoughts and other mental experiences arise, they have a cause that produces this effect. Usually the cause is quite similar to the effect. For example, one sad imprint that arises is the cause for a whole plethora of other sad or disturbing feelings and thoughts. The first one that arises produces an effect that becomes a cause of the next arising of a similar mental experience. In essence, we are endless arisings of causes and effects.

It is human nature to look for causes of events. If a young child contracts a terrible disease, we look for the cause. In part, we look for causes in order to find a solution to the problem. Oftentimes we look for the cause so we can alleviate our pain, or at least understand why the event is happening. We ask ourselves why an innocent being could suffer for no reason. If it isn't random, then we look to religious beliefs for the cause and ask ourselves, why is God punishing this pure being? We look to science and medicine for the cause, as well as the antidote. Some might say, "The universe brought this on for a reason." We might even arrogantly say, "It must be their karma. Accept it." While all of these ascribe a cause, none of them are really helpful.

I must be very clear: Karma is not synonymous with fate. Here are the basic tenets of karma, cause and effect, when used in Buddhist contexts:

1. Karma are seeds of potential that are stored in a person's mind or consciousness. They are mental in nature and formed by our mental activity.
2. These seeds are stored forever on one's mind and

they are produced by mental action: thoughts, feelings, emotions, and so on.

3. Karmic seeds are never lost until they are ripened or purified. Purified means we eliminate them so we do not need to experience their results.
4. In general, there are positive mental seeds and negative mental seeds. A positive, virtuous attitude produces a virtuous or wholesome seed. Wholesome seeds produce positive results. Negative seeds are produced by negative thoughts, emotions, and actions (actions that are accompanied by thoughts). Destructive thoughts are imprints that will produce destructive and painful experiences and feelings.
5. One can rid the mind of all negative imprints through the practice of meditation and other curative practices. Thus, karma is not fate. It is possible to change one's future, and the ultimate change is awakening.
6. Karmic imprints cannot be produced by someone else and then somehow transfer to another person's consciousness. The sins of our forebears are not ours to carry.

Reflection

As for all these reflections, begin by spending a few minutes settling the mind. With a rested sense of attention, reflect on how whatever arises must arise from a cause or arise randomly. If things arise randomly, then become convinced that anything could arise from anything else, even something wildly unrelated. Or perhaps things are just static? If things are static, that means they do not arise and fall away but are permanent and unchanging. Something permanent obviously cannot produce an effect. If it could, then the object would not be permanent. Does it really resonate for you that things happen randomly or that they are unchanging?

Now reflect on the possibility that things—physical events but particularly mental events—arise from a cause. If you're feeling depressed or anxious, doesn't everyone look for the cause? And if things are constantly in a state of flux, doesn't this indicate, even validate, that events arise from a cause?

Even deeper—and this takes a delicate and determined approach—everything we experience, we experience with the mind. In fact, all experience is really mental. When we are looking, hearing, smelling, tasting, or feeling, isn't that experience alone experienced within the mind? That is not to say that objects don't exist "out there," but the experience of that "out there" object, whether a sight, a smell, or anything else, is fully experienced within the mind. Furthermore, reflect on how if the object only existed "out there," then everyone would have the same experience of that object. Everyone would enjoy watching boxing, for example, or everyone would dislike it. The like or dislike of boxing really only occurs within the mindstream of each person. The same can be said about any object.

So that experience within the mind—whether pleasant, unpleasant, irritating, boring, blissful—is due to the mental imprints that were previously planted in one's consciousness.

Reflect on these ideas to the point where you can see that everything is experienced in the mind and that all mental experiences are tainted by our opinions, judgments, preferences, and so on from past experience. This line of thinking also should be concluded by an awareness that we have very little control over our mental processes, and thus are ruled by the past—our mental imprints, our karma.

Meditation

Now bring the focus deeper by focusing on the inhalation/exhalation at the nostrils or the rise and fall of the stomach. This time count to ten and then count backward to one, preferably for three rounds, which is best.

First, watch the arising of the thoughts, images, and impressions that are constantly arising in the mind. I find it especially effective to pay attention to a sound, even music, that you hear while you're sitting quietly. Notice how the sound occurred, and now watch the next thing that happens in the mind. What effect or result arose from the initial sound that entered your ear and then activated something in your mind? Let's say that irritation has arisen. That irritation is not embedded in the sound itself. That sound is the condition that now leads to a mental experience. If the sound is unpleasant to you, then that is because of an imprint planted on your consciousness that previously experienced and labeled that sound as unpleasant.

Without overanalyzing or conceptualizing, just watch this manifestation of an imprint arising, abiding, and falling away before it gives rise to the next mental experience. You could just as easily have had another experience besides irritation; with a different karmic seed, you could have another response, be it enjoyment or a pleasant sensation, since the music imprint planted on your consciousness earlier was an experience that was enjoyable.

Rest your focus into this process. You don't need to analyze anything. Just watch the mental experience and how its reaction is due to imprints you planted on your mind in the past. Watch dispassionately, without judgment. Let the one thought in your mind be your curiosity to discover how things are arising as a result of mental imprints.

13
Happiness

Topic

As we have discovered by now, the myth of happiness is the flip side of our real state of being. It's important to not become morbid here, though; the intent of understanding the *myth* of happiness is to know how we can attain *real* happiness. Happiness, we could say, is our birthright, and yet we just go from one problem to the next, one discomfort to the next, one unfulfilling or dissatisfying experience to the next.

The Buddha is often referred to in traditional literature as the true physician because he had knowledge and wisdom of how the mental afflictions, the "illnesses," arise and exist, and then clearly prescribed their remedies through teachings and practices. He attempted to wake us up to the fact that we are entitled to a much higher degree of happiness and fulfillment than what we are settling for. What we are settling for is labeled "suffering." The happiness we typically strive for leads to nothing more than a lack of fulfillment, a lack of liberation from an endless roller coaster of mental states.

What is the other side of this coin, then? In Buddhist literature, the word *happiness* is rarely used. Instead, the aim is portrayed as being "free" or "liberated" from problems. In this case, problems are primarily identified as mental problems, issues, disorders, and so forth, all of which are due to an uncontrolled mind. We are constantly at the whim of our emotions, our fears, our desires, our anxieties, and our disappointments. And while people will say, "That's life," they are unaware that there is a hidden diamond in the center of their hearts that, once accessed, will help them see that what they've been settling for is, well, crap.

Reflection

As for all these reflections, spend a few minutes settling the mind. Watch the inhalation and exhalation of the breath, either at the nostrils or at the stomach area. Do not try to change the breath in any way. Simple tune in to it, and by doing so you will have established a good basis for other kinds of gentle reflections.

Begin by gently reflecting on how you have been pursuing happiness from the time you were born up to today. Consider how your mind has led you to pursue objects of taste, feeling, smell, sensation, sight, and thought all for the purpose of feeling better or feeling pleasure. This would be acceptable if we just experienced the pleasure of the moment and let it go. But we do not let go. That "not letting go" is one indicator that just below the surface of the pleasure or discomfort is our actual state of being—imbalance, discomfort, dis-ease. If we were in a state of ease, in the long term or sustaining sense, we would have no need to be constantly moving to entertain ourselves, to stimulate our senses once the previous stimulant begins to fade away. Next, you can reflect on how none of your sources of "happiness" or pleasure last for more than a few minutes. You then spend your time attempting to regain that sense of ease once it has faded, so your natural, unfortunate state is one of dis-ease and discomfort. You may not be conscious that this is how you pursue happiness, but that is itself the point of this reflection.

Finally, reflect upon how your roller coaster, uncontrolled mind has never given you lasting satisfaction or liberated you from suffering. As Lama Yeshe used to say, we are like a cow with a ring through its nose, attached to a rope that pulls us wherever the mind thinks it will be satisfied.

Meditation

Now bring the focus a little deeper by counting to ten with each breath and then counting backward to one. If you can do this for three rounds, that is best.

Try to zero in on a feeling you got from your contemplation in the reflection above. Try to feel it or see it in a nonconceptional way. See how there is this constant sense of grasping, eternally, for satisfaction. Zero in and hold it without too much tightness or too much slack in your attention. Allow that feeling to reveal itself to you while you maintain a state of watchfulness. Don't interpret whether this or that route to happiness might still be at least partially valid—none of that. Just watch. Just experience the grasping.

There may come a moment where you intuitively see it for what it is: "That is suffering." That endless quest for comfort is an unsettled state, and thus a trap, like a prison disguised as an exciting place to be—an amusement park you're locked inside of and can never leave. This "anti-happiness" has always fooled us into thinking it is happiness. Experience this; the experience is a "knowing." Focus on this knowing and allow it to reveal whatever lessons are there for you, without purposefully thinking about or intellectualizing it. This kind of learning is intuitive and experiential, and thus deep; it develops the mind in a new way. Stay in that experience as long as you can without squeezing it. When the experience begins to fade, see if you can regenerate it. When you're unable to do so any longer, then be content with what you've accomplished and go on with your day.

14
You Only Live Once

Topic

The natural, everyday mindset of people is to just go about their lives without any consideration or awareness that there is more to their existence than just this lifetime. This default awareness of ours is even more striking when we consider our recent past and how we just stumble along as if this is all there is and nothing continues on after it. However, when we consider the nature of the mind, how our consciousness is ever-changing, going from one cause-and-effect sequence to the next, we see our "self" as in a flow rather than a solid monolith. In this never-ending flow, every effect creates another cause. So, at the end of life, this process of flow—this arising, abiding, ceasing, and abiding—does not stop. The nature of the mind itself is unending.

Reflection

As for the other reflections, spend a few minutes settling the mind. Just watch the inhalation and exhalation of the breath through the nostrils. If the mind is very unsettled, then you can watch the breath at the stomach area going in and out. Do this twenty-one times, with each exhalation counting as one, staying focused in order to not lose count.

Now, with a gentle mind, reflect on the progression of your life and how you've been the same person who has evolved throughout your life. See your life as a flow of film rather than a collection of various photographs. Get a feeling for this constant flow from your past.

Meditation

Bring the focus a little deeper by focusing on the inhalation/exhalation at the nostrils, or stomach if that's more comfortable. This time count to ten and then count backward to one for three rounds, if possible.

Now settle into watching the mind. Watch the thoughts, feelings, sounds, and images that come up, whatever is in your field of mental experience at the present moment. After a moment or two, regress backward to the thought before the present thought, the feeling before the present feeling, the sensation or image that led to the present one. Now, regress a little further back to a few minutes before that chain arose, and see the thoughts that preceded the next ones and actually helped create the ones after them. After that, you can go back a few hours. Go slowly, paying attention to all the arisings and fallings and arisings that have led to the present moment. See how they are all connected, and how one moment creates the immediately subsequent one. This must be experiential, just like watching an engaging movie in which your conceptual thinking mind is quiet and you are just in the experience. Become familiar with the experience.

Now keep doing your regression by seamlessly following the process to the day before, and then the day before that. Then go back a week. Now jump, without losing purpose, back a month, a year, a decade. See the various thoughts and images of this stream as interconnected causes and effects leading up to the present moment. Now go back to being an infant. Can you find the beginning there? You cannot, because there is no beginning but just a series of arisings, abidings, ceasings, and arisings. Now, with an experiential and curious mindset, see if this series started in the womb. It did not. Using your imagination, gently try to see the thoughts, the mental movement that existed before your consciousness entered the fertilized egg in your mother's womb. You may get a strong sense of conviction of the unendingness of your consciousness, such that you can feel that experience deeply in a visceral way, like an aha moment. Then, strongly but gently focus on this aha! so that it becomes a full body and mental experience, a complete perception you are familiar with.

While maintaining your focus and the experience of the unending stream of consciousness, of the continuous flow of cause-effect-cause, bring your awareness back to the present and to your sense of how you exist. Now, with your imagination, but without getting lost or distracted in thought, observe where your consciousness will be in ten minutes. Then from there, follow it to the end of the day and to the next morning, through your sleep. Continue to ride the consciousness like this—imagining your thoughts or images or whatever resonates—all the way up until the end of your life. Of course, this is imaginative, but it is rooted in reality. You will reach the end of this life. But then what happens to the momentum of this rising of cause and effect, of this stream of ever-flowing thoughts, images, feelings, and experiences? See how you are absorbed into the reality of dying. What happens at the very last moment? Well, the last moment is another cause that will lead to another effect. So your consciousness, now extremely subtle, leaves your body and continues onward. It is "thrown" into another fertilized egg, and now the process carries on. If you like, you can watch it through the germination phase and on to your birth, your early development, and so on. The important thing here is that you get the experiential insight of the never-ending flow of consciousness so that you can become convinced that the myth of only living once is just that—a myth.

About the Author

For over thirty years, Karuna Cayton worked as a licensed psychotherapist, business psychologist, and coach to help people achieve a more balanced life. When he was twenty years old, he moved to Nepal, where he lived and worked for twelve years. In Nepal he studied and practiced Tibetan Buddhism at Kopan Monastery with Lama Yeshe and Lama Zopa Rinpoche. Karuna is the author of *The Misleading Mind: How We Create Our Own Problems and How Buddhist Psychology Can Help Us Solve Them*. He has dedicated his life to explaining the deep teachings of Buddhism and their relevance for everyday people.

What to Read Next from Wisdom Publications

A Monk's Guide to Finding Joy
How to Train Your Mind and Transform Your Life
His Eminence Khangser Rinpoche

"*A Monk's Guide to Finding Joy* is a heartfelt invitation to a path of self-discovery and transformation. For anyone seeking a roadmap to genuine happiness based on the clarity, power, and depths of Buddhist teachings, this book is an invaluable companion on the journey!" —Tara Brach, author of *Radical Acceptance* and *Trusting the Gold*

The Power of Meditation
A Complete Guide to Transforming Your Mind
Lama Zopa Rinpoche

In *The Power of Meditation*, Lama Zopa Rinpoche offers clear explanations and instructions for the life-changing practice of meditation.

About Wisdom Publications

Wisdom Publications is the leading publisher of classic and contemporary Buddhist books and practical works on mindfulness. To learn more about us or to explore our other books, please visit our website at wisdom.org or contact us at the address below.

Wisdom Publications
132 Perry Street
New York, NY 10014 USA

We are a 501(c)(3) organization, and donations in support of our mission are tax deductible.

Wisdom Publications is affiliated with the Foundation for the Preservation of the Mahayana Tradition (FPMT).